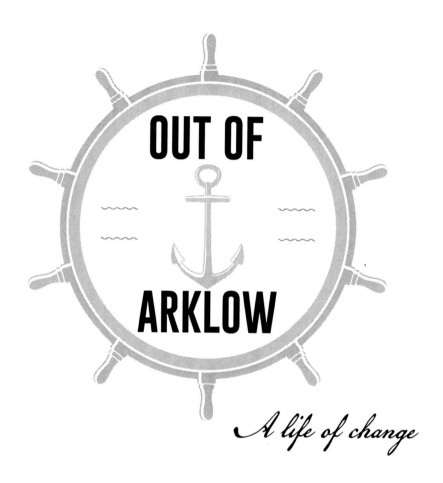

OUT OF

ARKLOW

A life of change

DANNY O'NEILL

authorHOUSE®

AuthorHouse™ UK Ltd.
1663 Liberty Drive
Bloomington, IN 47403 USA
www.authorhouse.co.uk
Phone: 0800.197.4150

Published by AuthorHouse 03/27/2014

ISBN: 978-1-4918-9599-3 (sc)
ISBN: 978-1-4918-9595-5 (hc)
ISBN: 978-1-4918-9600-6 (e)

Contents

FOREWORD

I FIRST SAILED out of Arklow as a boy on the fishing boats, going from boy to ordinary seaman (OS) on small coasters. I then joined the Shipping Federation in Liverpool as OS and efficient deck hand (EDH) on tramps, tankers and coasters. Following this, I sat my 2nd Mates and served as 2nd mate on cattle boats and 3rd mate on cross channel passenger boats. Then I went foreign on tramp steamers as 3rd and 2nd Mate.

After that I served as mate and master of coastal tramps, chief officer on tankers and Very Large Crude Carriers (VLCCs), Oil Bulk Ore ships (OBOs), master on tankers, container vessels, coastal tramps, survey ships, tugs, fishery patrol boat and dredgers. I served as harbour master and pilot, sailed and delivered yachts and boats.

In total I served on eighty different types of craft in positions ranging from boy to master, not including yachts and boats or the many ships I have piloted in and out of Arklow. Out of these 80 vessels I served as master of thirty-seven of them.

Over my career, I have carried numerous types of cargoes, including coal, coke, timber, tree trunks, Christmas trees, peat moss, sugar, grain, phosphates, animal feed, newsprint, paper pulp, scrap, pit props, china clay, rail tracks, steel ingots, steel pipes, steel sheets, steel rods, steel rolls, cattle, sheep, pigs, horses, sulphur, whisky, malt, hops, Guinness, stones, crude oil, gasoline, mogas, aviation fuel, kerosene, naphtha, chemicals in bulk, chemicals in road tankers, bombs, guns, gunturrants, ammunition, rocket launchers, airplanes, hover craft, stators, generators, nuclear waste, bullion, meat, fruit, vegetables, butter, milk, produce, chocolates, passengers, fish, motor cars, caravans, trucks, tractors, combine harvesters, dumpers, bulldozers, yachts, landing craft, troops, hides, esparto grass, NAAFI stores and containers which could contain almost anything.

CHAPTER 1

Growing Up in Arklow

I FIRST WENT to sea on a professional (or paid) basis at the age of thirteen, but it seems to me that I have being going to sea all my life. My first memory of the dock in Arklow goes back to when, at age three, I almost drowned while sailing a little homemade boat in its murky waters. I remember reaching out with a long stick to free the little boat that had become foul of some debris. The next thing I remember is waking up in my Aunt Annie's bed. It turned out that I had overreached and toppled into the dock. My companion, who was a couple of years older than me, started screaming and shouting, alerting a group of fishermen who were talking together at the far corner of the dock. Fortunately for me, it was a fine Sunday morning, meaning that they were not at sea. When they arrived at the scene some minutes later, there was no sign of me and, being fishermen, not one of them could swim. They then searched some fishing boats for a long boathook, as I was in about seven feet of water and invisible in the dirty murk. They prodded the bottom with the boathook until they found and hooked me. After they hauled me up on the quay they caused me somehow to spew up the water I had swallowed and carried me to my grandmother's house, which was, and still is, only about three hundred meters from where I fell in and this is where I came to, in bed. As it was a Sunday morning my parents were in mass and, by the time they heard about the incident, I was out and about again.

I vaguely remember falling in, struggling and then waking up in bed. Most of what I have written here was told by my cousin and by my rescuers who, over the years to come, I would meet many a time around the dockside, all of whom have now gone to their just reward. May they all rest in peace.

The toy boat, which I almost lost my life over, was made out of half a flat cork float taken from the headline of a herring driftnet. The cork was cut in half long ways down the middle, rubbed on a cement wall until the bow and stern was sharpened and formed to your personal satisfaction. A slot was then cut with a sharp knife fore and aft along the bottom of the hull. Then, into the slot, you would insert a piece of Bangor roof slate for a deep keel. This keel, no longer just a piece of slate, was held in place by the friction and pressure of the cork hull acting on both sides. Then the masts and sails were shaped. The masts were made out of a piece of wood, pared by a knife to a point and stuck vertically into the hull. The sails were the easiest to rig and to replace. They were simply a piece of cardboard cut from a cigarette packet and slipped down the masts by cutting two small holes in the sails for that purpose. Sails could be square or fore and aft and could be adjusted to steer the boat, taking note of the wind direction, to a particular point across the dock which was normally the easiest place to recover it.

Races were held that took into account the speed and direction. The first boat to arrive at a finish line about fifteen feet wide was the winner. Any boat that was outside the finish line was disqualified. Needless to say, at the age of three, I was far too young to shape my own boats, so I must assume that it was made for me by one of my older cousins.

During the years of World War II when I was growing up, conditions were very poor in Ireland. In the early years of the war, England had not yet geared itself up with regards equipment and ships to fight a total war. It was being hit badly at sea due to the sinking of its ships by German submarines, which threatened to cut off its supply lines of raw materials and foodstuffs.

Ireland was caught without a proper foreign-going merchant fleet. It had mostly been dependent on British ships to supply its needs, but now found itself in a desperate state, left without enough ships to supply the country, while British ships were all involved in supplying much-needed material and food to its own people and contributing towards the war effort.

Before the outbreak of the war Ireland had a few coastal and cross-channel vessels under the Irish flag, but not nearly enough to meet its needs, there were no foreign-going ships under the Irish flag. However, there were a large number of Irish seamen of all ranks sailing under the British and other foreign flags.

In order to make up a fleet of foreign-going ships the Irish government was compelled to purchase any tonnage which would come onto the market in order to supply its needs of foreign foodstuffs and materials. They began by buying or chartering ships that were laid up in various ports, due to their home countries having been overrun and controlled by the Nazi regime.

Arklow had about ten schooners of an average of about one hundred and fifty ton lifting capacity each, which before the war, had been more than enough to cater for its needs and had spent much of the time laid up for lack of cargoes. Some of the older schooners and ketches had been stripped of their rigging, masts, sails and other gear to enable the best of them to continue trading. In other words, the older boats were cannibalized for the sake of the others and were left derelict in the harbour together with a lot of fishing smacks that were unable to ply their trade for various reasons, such as the scarcity of oil or gear due to the war.

The river in the 40s

Arklow dock in the 40s

The needs created by the war gave the Arklow fleet a new lease of life. Cargoes that had been scarce before the war, due to competition from British and Dutch better-equipped ships, were now there for the taking as there was now not enough ships to go around.

Although Ireland was neutral, it could not but be effected by the war being waged all around it. Arklow was particularly badly hit as almost every house in the town had some person at sea, mostly serving in British ships, and hardly a week passed without some house receiving word that a member of the family was reported missing at sea.

Apart from the fact that basics were very hard to find and most were rationed, it was a great time to grow up in Arklow. For those of us interested in boats, water, beaches, big sand dunes, rocks and rivers, it was heaven, and we made the most of it. We were allowed great freedom and as soon as we were able to dump our schoolbags at home, we were off to some place.

There was always something going on down the quays. Fishing boats would be departing or landing and we took pride in being the first to name a boat as it approached the pier head, at a distance of about five miles. We were also able to name the skipper and most of the crew. They were, for the most part, friends, neighbours or relations.

We were allowed to help out in the fishing boats and we were always on board, if possible, when they were shifting berths or going out on trials. The seasonal change in fishing meant a good deal of activity and work. In October, just before Halloween, some boats would be changing over from trawling to either long lining or drifting for herrings.

Both long lines and drift nets would require coating or barking before use. This was done by filling a large iron *barking pot,* of about one hundred gallon capacity or more, with water. Into this pot was placed very brittle lumps of cutch (a brown dye from tree bark, used for tanning and preserving nets, ropes and sails), broken from a large slab which was purchased from the local hardware and boat supplies store. Under the pot a large fire was built and the water heated and boiled until the cutch melted. The pot was kept on the boil and the nets, lines, ropes, sails or anything else that might need coating was soaked in the concoction until they were thoroughly soaked through. This operation was necessary to help preserve the gear from the harsh environment in which it was soon going to be exposed.

Barking always reminded me of cooking up a witch's brew, with all the smoke from the wood and coal fire, the steam from the boiling pot and all the bodies in attendance, dressed in all sorts of rough clothing and footwear for protection against the inevitable splashes from the boiling brown mixture.

The youngsters were involved in helping out, doing odd jobs, darting in and out, topping up the pot with water and keeping the fire fed. I always remember being sorted out for punishment in school after a session of barking when our teacher accused me of smoking cigarettes and gave me six of his best because he detected brown stains between my fingers. He came from the midlands and was not familiar with our methods of working.

With the introduction of synthetic nets, ropes and lines in the late 1950s, that did not require preservation as did the older hemp, cotton, and manila gear, the barking pots began to disappear.

Each boat owner had a pony, or donkey and cart for the purpose of hauling gear or equipment to and from the boats to the net sheds and it was always the boy's job to catch the animal, yoke it to the cart, water and feed it, and drive it as required. They were used for other reasons as well, such as hauling sand, shifting household furnishings, collecting fuel from the woods and sawdust to feed the stoves, known as *Nellie Kellies* or *Cossors*.

I do not know why they were called *Nelly Kellies*. I suspect they were called after the popular song at the time called *'The Daughter of Officer Kelly'*, that ended with the words *'Nelly Kelly I love you'*. They certainly were a lifesaver during the war years when it was hard for us to get coal fuel due to shipping shortages. The *Nelly Kelly* was constructed by getting a five gallon (25-litre) oil drum and cutting the top off it. A two inch diameter hole was then cut in the centre of the bottom. The drum was then placed on three bricks and packed full with dry sawdust with a broom handle down through the middle of the sawdust and out through the hole in the bottom. With the saw dust packed tight the broom handle was removed and the *Nelly Kelly* lighted from the bottom. The bricks allowed the air under the drum and the hole acted as a funnel to create a draft to keep the sawdust burning. With a well-packed drum it could burn for up to twenty-four hours. A large pot of water on top could keep the household in boiling water for all its uses. Each house normally had two *Nellies*, one in use, and the other ready for use and they were operated in the backyard under cover.

All the donkeys and ponies were allowed to graze free range on the golf course and, when they saw us coming to collect them, they would always lead us a merry chase until we could manage to corner them and get a rope on them.

During the war and for some years after it, the fishing fleet in Arklow was made up of a very mixed selection of boats of sizes varying from twenty to fifty feet in length and various ages, from being reasonably new up to seventy years old. Some of those older boats had been built for either rowing or sailing and it was only in later years that engines were fitted. There was a large variety of engines throughout the fleet, which were received and fitted when they became available, with little choice as to the make or horse power. For this reason, some of the smaller boats were overpowered and some of the larger boats underpowered. Two engine makes come to mind, the Dan and the Bolinder engines. All of them had one thing in common; they were what were called *hot pot engines*. This meant that there was a heavy iron pot on each cylinder which had to be heated until it was glowing red before the engine would fire. This was achieved by directing blowlamps or blowtorches onto each hot pot, until they glowed red and at that point the engine was turned over, which caused the injector to spray a jet of gas oil under the red hot pots which exploded the gas in the cylinders and forced the pistons down a stroke. This was done in turn with all cylinders until the engine gained enough momentum and fired itself. When that point was reached the engineer stopped turning the engine and the blowtorches were removed and turned off. Some engines were slower to start than others and some had starting handles, while the smaller ones had a rope that you would wind around the flywheel and pull, similar to an outboard.

There was one boat, which, for reasons of space, did not allow a starting handle to be fitted and was started by means of two men walking then running in their stocking feet on the flywheel. One man lay down on one side of the flywheel and pushed with his feet to get it turning and the other person stood upright on the other side of the wheel first walking it and then running in small steps. They had stout grips built into the engine room to give them leverage and to haul themselves out of danger when they finally reached a rate which was sufficient to turn and fire the engine. When the war ended and they received a new engine, they both put on a lot of weight due to the lack of exercise!

Another fisherman bought a forty-five foot deep keeled yacht and converted her into a fishing boat. Her engine was not powerful enough to tow a trawl so, after stripping her mid-ship saloon of all its beautiful mahogany woodwork and brass fittings, and converting it into a fish hold, fitted an extra engine to supplement the original and increase the horse power. As the yacht's engine was installed forward on the centre line there was no other place for the second engine but alongside the original with the shaft running aft parallel to the original shaft and exiting the hull to one side of the stern post. This worked quite well and the boat fished successfully until, with her deep keel, she grounded while entering port on the notoriously shifting sands of the bar of Arklow and became a constructive total loss. However, because of the tight space in and around the second engine, starting it was a bit of a problem. The method of starting was to wrap a few turns of a rope around an attachment on the flywheel and pull it, similar to that of an outboard engine. This starting procedure worked well, except when the starting line became stuck and did not release itself from the flywheel when the engine fired. The end of the starting line, with its large knot, would start flogging the operator, who was unable to move in his tight working space with all its moving parts. He would have to curl into a ball for protection while the rope beat him on the back as he screamed for somebody to stop the engine.

Another boat with a similar starting procedure, but with a much bigger engine, developed a method of starting it by using the pony to pull the starting line. They cut a hole in the deck directly above the flywheel and led a line down the hole. A wooden plug with the line attached was inserted into a hole in the flywheel. A few turns was taken around the flywheel, the line was led ashore through a system of pulleys and hooked onto a harness on the pony on the quay wall. The pony was then given a slap on the rump and, as she took off, she pulled the rope which turned the wheel which fired the engine. It worked very well, except on one occasion, when I remember the plug getting stuck in the flywheel and the engine began to haul the pony back to the boat. Somebody cut the rope but the poor pony must have got a bit of a fright for she took off up the quay wall and it took us some time to capture her again.

Another boat's reverse gear broke down and the owner was unable to get spares due to the war, so he managed to bypass the problem which left the boat with only forward propulsion. He solved this by turning off the engine when approaching the berth and having two large sweeps managed to manoeuvre the boat in.

Looking back, all of the above seems to be rather comical, but those people were good fishermen and workers. Before the war these men had fished as far away as the Shetland Islands. They knew all the fishing grounds around the coast of Ireland and the Isle of Man. They had been employed by the government to teach practical methods of fishing to the people of the west by taking their boats around there and giving them hands-on experience. During the war years they simply could not get equipment or spares. If something broke or wore out they had to compromise and make do with what was on hand, or do without.

I remember, as one of the many young boys about the boats at that time, we used to collect the waste crankcase lubricating oil from the fishermen. We then sold it on to an enterprising Jewish man who added some perfumed concoction to it and passed it off as hair oil which he sold to barber shops.

It was not until 1948 that new boats came on line again. These were the *Fifty-Footers,* which were built around the coast in places such as Arklow, Killybegs, Baltimore and Meevagh. Designed and subsidised by An Board Iascaigh Mhara (BIM), which was previously known as the Irish Sea Fisheries Association (ISFA), they were multi-purpose boats and, when built, the Fisheries Board handed them over to experienced fishermen on very reasonable terms.

When the war ended and, in the late 1940s and early 50s, materials and equipment became available again, these fishermen, with the aid of government grants, invested in new and bigger boats and continued to thrive until we joined the European Common Market and the government sold out the fishermen to fatten the farmers.

When the drift-netting season was over and the boats were changed back to trawling the cotton herring nets had to be completely dried before being stowed away in the net loft until next season. This was done by spreading the miles of the cotton herring nets in the grass and over the sand dunes by flaking them out over the back of the cart pulled by the pony.

The fishermen had returned to sea so the nets were looked after by retired men and the boys. It was a community affair as the nets had to be turned over and shook regularly and one shower of rain would undo days of care. Even when dried and being stowed away the dust off the nets contained a fair bit of dried jelly fish which could still irritate.

The boats involved in long lining were called *Hookers* because they caught their catch by hooking them. They normally used seven lines, and each line had three hundred and sixty cod hooks, each hook was baited with a whelk.

One other attraction for the boys was going out on the Hookers on Saturday mornings to lift the pots that were used to fish for whelks which were then were used to bait the long lines. The whelks were caught in a string of woven basket type pots. Each pot was baited with a half rotten dog fish. The pots were lifted, emptied, re-baited and thrown overboard to fish again. The whelks were then broken on a flat stone using a large wooden mallet and supplied to the baiters who sat beside their lines, baited each hook and coiled the line in a specially designed box, which was called a trock, in such a way as to enable the line to run clear without fouling any one of the three hundred and sixty baited hooks in the same trock as the boat sped ahead through the water.

Shooting the lines took a fair bit of skill and I have to admit that I became quite good at it. There was a certain amount of art in shooting and it was essential that you built up a rhythm with your arms so that you could throw the hooks clear of the boat and work at the same speed as the boat over the ground. Lines were shot while running with the tide. This was because the tide would help to stretch the lines along the bottom. With the very strong tides running outside the Arklow banks, it was impossible to stop the boat and there was always a man standing by, close to you, with a knife, ready to cut the line in case of foul-ups.

Having said all this, it was not all work and no play for the youth of Arklow. At the end of the war, and some years after it the population was still on war rations. We had never seen a banana or an orange. Flour and sugar, when you could get it, was brown. Cigarettes were sold in ones and twos. Chocolate was unavailable. But, what we never had we never missed, and everyone I knew was in the same boat. We got on with enjoying ourselves.

There was a control price placed by the government on the sale of fish which meant that fish could not be sold by the fishermen above that price. This was meant to keep the price of fish down during the food shortages, which was good for the people, but it did the fishermen no favours, especially since the government did not lift the restrictive price until well into the 1950s.

As there was a fair amount of auxiliary schooners visiting and owned in Arklow and a lot more beyond use laid up in the river there was plenty for young boys to do. We would dare each other to climb the ratlines to the top of the masts, or to dive from the highest point. We would launch the open lifeboats of the schooners, which were normally swung over the side while they were working cargo, which made it easy. But even if the boats were not swung out, we occasionally launched them from their stowed position on the hatch, much to the annoyance of the skipper and the night watchman.

We played pirates on the derelict vessels and sent boarders across in requisitioned boats to overwhelm the imaginary crews. We rowed the boats out through the piers and into the beaches where many times we were caught in a falling tide and had to remain there until the next tide floated us off.

I have to say that we never intentionally damaged a boat. We did take chances and annoyed a lot of people but we were all too involved in the seagoing life around us to purposely do harm. But we did do some damage on occasion.

When an old schooner reached the end of its life and there was nothing left of any value on board, and while the hull below the waterline was still reasonably intact, the owner would decide that it was time to take her on her last voyage to sea. A local fishing boat, the Willing Lass, would tow the hulk out when it floated on a spring tide and when the wind was blowing from the east. She would then let the tow go at the most convenient rocks on shore and hopefully let the wind and tide do the rest. I remember two boats that missed the rocks and were driven ashore on the sandy beaches where they eventually broke up after some time and with the help of some locals with saws. These abandoned and broken vessels were a Godsend to us where we were able to let our imaginations run riot and which we used as diving platforms until they eventually disintegrated. The schooners that I remember being disposed of in this manner were the Harvest King, the Tarragona, the Uncle Ned, the KT, and the Agnes Craig. The M.E. Johnson was lost on the beach directly behind the south pier some years later, while attempting to make an entry into the harbour in bad weather.

Another favourite pastime of ours was to take a boat up the river and poach salmon and trout. We all considered that it was as much our river as it was Lord Wicklow's.

Directly across the river from the dock entrance was what looked like a bombed out site with large and high walls, skeletons of buildings, large holes, tunnels and old derelict jetties. It was a marvellous place for boys to play war games and cowboys and Indians. The site covered an area of approximately one square mile and was once occupied by the Kynocks Ammunition Factory, which was owned by the Chamberlain family in England and employed up to 1000 local people. For the duration of hostilities, between 1914 and 1918, Kynochs employed four thousand workers, bussed and trained in from surrounding towns. Because of its nature, the factory buildings were well spaced and all were built between banks of sand to deflect any explosion. Buildings were connected by narrow entries, tunnels and a small rail system. When the factory suffered a big accidental explosion in 1917, killing many workers, the owners decided, due to the uncertain political situation at the time, to re-site in Umbogintwini in South Africa.

Since 1918, when the company pulled out, the site was allowed to deteriorate and overgrow and become a warren for rabbits, from which incidentally some locals made a few pounds during the war years, trapping rabbits for consumption at home and in the U.K. This was a place of fascination for us. We could let our imagination run wild. It could be Dracula land, or cowboy and Indian land, pirate and war territory, and among the ruins there were explosives waiting for us to dig up. Buried under the ruins were large quantities of guncotton. As youngsters we dug it up, smuggled it home and secretly dried it out in the range when mom wasn't looking, or if the weather was fine, dried it out in the sun. We made bombs by packing the guncotton tightly into steel or copper pipes and sealing each end by hammering and leaving a fuse out of a small opening. Sometimes we threw a sealed *bomb* into a fire and waited for the inevitable explosion.

It was a highly dangerous game and I shudder to think what might have happened. I can only remember one accident, when a bomb in an open fire was taking too long to explode and one of us went up to the fire to check if all was working when the bomb went off. Fortunately he was not close enough to do himself any great damage but for a while there was some fear that he would lose an eye but they were able to save it. He was left with a scar on his face for life. Needless to say, our parents lived in fear for us and warned us against visiting the Kynochs ruins. But, to go swimming on the North Beach we had to pass through the old factory. It was wide open for everyone.

On the dunes and Green beside the harbour, where we dried and mended the nets before we put them away, we played football, hurley, rounders, tug of war, and golf. You may wonder how we came to play golf. In 1927, a golf links was developed among the sand dunes, stretching for over a mile along the coast south of the harbour. As the *Links* was naturally full of hills and hollows, the then well-to-do golfers needed someone to carry their golf bags around the course.

This was when the caddies came in to being. In 1944/45, when I joined the caddy bank, the *Links* was well-established and a type of caddies union had formed. This was to keep the caddy business in the fishery area of the town. As caddies, we were given old golf clubs by golf club members that we caddied for. We were also allowed to play on the course on Saturday mornings and eventually we arranged an annual caddies' competition. This worked out very well for all involved. As caddies we were able to earn some money when money was a very scarce commodity, it passed the time, gave us another interest, kept us off the one street (where everyone knew everyone else) and we kept a good eye on the course, which was not fenced in at the time, by driving cows, horses, donkeys and goats off the greens.

Years afterwards, while still at sea, I became a life member of the same golf club, which has improved vastly over the years. The old course layout can clearly be observed from the vantage point of my house which is built above the old caddy bank, overlooking the course with a panoramic view of the harbour, the piers, the bay, the river, the beach and the rocks where the schooners were laid to rest. I have come full circle.

Scene at Arklow Harbour in the 1940s

CHAPTER 2

The Fishing Vessel, Erin's Hope

ALTHOUGH I HAD already been away on the fishing vessel, the Saint Michael, during my summer school holidays, my first official seagoing job at age thirteen was in the Erin's Hope. She was a typical 50-foot, wooden, general-purpose fishing boat. She was built by Jack Tyrrell in Arklow and launched in 1949. She was engaged mainly in drift netting for herrings in summer, long lining or hooking in winter, trawling in between times. Then, with the development of sounders and fish finders, she changed from long lining and drifting to seine netting, or ringing, as it was called locally, with seven coils of two and a half inch manila ropes, each side using a rope coiler and a seine net.

I almost lost my life taking a coil of rope away from the coiler in bad weather when she took a heavy roll and threw me over the side. Luckily the skipper, Sam Dixon, saw me going over and immediately stopped the propeller. I went over the port shoulder and the crew naturally looked for me on that side but I had gone right under the boat and came up on the starboard side. My shouts alerted the skipper in the wheelhouse and I was soon pulled back on board. Had he not knocked the propeller off it may have been a different story. I was wearing heavy white thigh-length sea boots and an overall fisherman's smock and feared that I would not last very long. Luckily air trapped in the smock counteracted the weight of the heavy water-filled boots and brought me back to the surface after dragging me along the keel for a short distance.

I was engaged as cook and boy on half a share, which was the normal way that boys were taken on when starting off their careers.

The Erin's Hope carried four men when engaged in trawling and seven when engaged in the herring drifting, ringing and while long lining. I was also expected to lend a hand on board doing almost anything when required. I was there to learn the job.

The worst job of all was coiling the foot line when drifting for herring, where I spent the whole time while hauling the nets in the locker below and under the deck winch, coiling the heavy, tarred, three-inch manila rope. The rope came down through a hole in the deck directly over my head and in the summer time, when the jelly fish were numerous, there was a steady stream of jelly fish slime and streamers wrapped around the rope, cascading down on me working under the hole in the deck.

In July, August and September the jellyfish, or *skarrigs*, as they were known locally, matured and developed long colourful streamers about two meters long trailing out of them. Those three months were the most painful and agonizing. The fallout from the jelly fish streamer was torturous and everyone on board suffered from it, but not as much as the boy in the locker. It took hours to wear off and everything you touched you transferred it on. It made you itch like you had never itched before. It was on your hands, wrists, face, in your hair and down your neck. It got into your bed, your nose, and eyes and when you went to the toilet it got up your rectum, onto your penis and you itched and itched. There was no use washing for you only spread it around.

Cooking for seven men on a single-ring coal-fired bogie in the cabin which also slept the whole crew was no joke, even in port while the boat was steady, but when being tossed around at sea and being seasick with the smell of food, oil, bilge water and body odours, it was something else.

Everyone on board worked on a share basis and on the Arklow boats it all depended on how many men were on board, and that depended on the type of fishing you were engaged in. With four men there were eight shares and with seven men there were fourteen shares, always double the amount of people working on board. Shares were worked out after all expenses were deducted from the gross earnings such as fuel, food, cigarettes and sundries. The skipper was on two shares, the first hand on one and a half shares and the rest of the crew on one share each, except for the boy on half a share. When trawling with four men this worked out at a total of eight shares paid out to those on board and the remaining two shares went to the owner who paid off the boat and supplied the gear and equipment

To my knowledge, the Erin's Hope was one of the last boats to be engaged in mid-water herring drifting off the Isle of Man and elsewhere. This was because of the development of the Scottish herring ringers, seine nets, vinge trawls, fish finders, rope coilers and more powerful engines. The risk to long trains of drift nets hanging like curtains just below the surface in busy shipping lanes, from the continuing increase in commercial shipping, also helped in the decline of the drifting for herring. This made the drifters shift to areas only where shipping was light and eventually the offshore drifting for herrings ceased altogether.

In the early 1950s these types of fishing boats were not fitted with any electronic equipment. When the Erin's Hope was launched in 1949, she was fitted only with twelve volt lighting for cabin and navigation illumination. She was also supplied with a full set of sails by the builders, a fore sail, a leg of mutton main sail and a mizzen-gaff sail. Most boats launched prior to this period were fitted only with oil lamps and obviously the engines were still not trusted.

The Pye medium range trawler band radio was the first modern instrument fitted and at the beginning was used mainly for entertainment. Next came the echo sounder which, at the start, would only tell the depth of water and the bottom contour directly under the hull and printed the findings on a paper roll. It was not until about two decades later that the modern fish-finder made its appearance.

I joined her in June 1950, as boy and cook, to go herring fishing off the Isle of Man, and landing in Howth. On arrival back in Arklow, in August, I was sent back to school to finish my education in the Boys National School, which was compulsory until I reached the age of fourteen, when I left full-time education to join the fishing boat, the Saint Michael.

The Saint Michael was built as a sailing fishing boat at the turn of the century and later fitted with a small engine. She was forty-five feet long and was engaged in drifting, long lining and trawling. She had no electronics of any description, only a coal-fuelled bogie, a flare, made up of a round net cork float, wrapped in a diesel oil-soaked bunch of rags on the end of a steel rod, and oil lamps for illumination.

The homemade flare was for emergencies but used mainly to warn other craft of our drift nets. We carried no pyrotechnics, no life raft, no life jackets, and no radio; just this homemade flare. No wonder the poor women spent most of their time on the pier head looking out for us.

CHAPTER 3

Arklow Lifeboat in the 1950s

IT WAS TRADITIONAL in those days for local fishermen to become members of the local life boat. There was always a large amount of volunteers on the books. I imagine the reason for this was that there would always be a fair amount of the men away from home at any one time and, in this way, there would always be enough men available ashore, for whatever reason, to man the boat. They were mostly fishermen also, because it was considered that if you could do a fisherman's job you were good enough for the lifeboat. There was very little extra training required and you received the training as you helped man the lifeboat on sea trials.

The main difference between the lifeboat and the fishing craft in those days was that the lifeboat was better maintained and equipped with lifesaving gear and oilskins and she was safer and more reliable. There was not much difference in the handling of the boats as there were no electronics on board either, so therefore there was not a great lot to learn. The main difference was the equipment carried on board, learning to use it and familiarizing the crew as to where it was stowed and learning the drill.

The fishermen lived close to the dockside and the lifeboat. In the days before motor cars, television sets, loud music, telephones and bleepers were in common usage, it was essential that the volunteers lived close enough to the boat to hear the call when the maroons went off and had to run down to the lifeboat station. To avoid delays the first seven men down to the boathouse grabbed the oilskins and boots and boarded the boat while the following people manned the house, opened the big doors, lifted the steel bridge and, when everything was shipshape and the boat's engines were running the order was given to release the hook. With that a man would tap the pin with a hammer and the boat would slide down the slip and into the water. As soon as she hit the water the rudder was lowered, the mast was raised and the engines were put on full ahead. No radar scanner or aerials to worry about, there were none.

Arklow lifeboat, 1950

From 1952 to December 1954 I was back in the Erin's Hope, to a modernized boat having been fitted with a Pye radio medium range transmitter radio, a Kelvin Hughes paper roller type echo sounder and wire rope bridles or warps for trawling. It was the usual seasonal work, hooking or long lining in winter, trawling in the spring and seine netting or ringing in summer and autumn. There was no more drifting for herrings.

After a very poor long lining season in the winter of 1954, which resulted in a disastrous Christmas holiday, financially, I decided to alter my career and look for a job in the coastal trade on one of the Arklow Coasters. At that time, in early 1955 there was a choice of coasters and schooners owned in Arklow and there was always a changeover of personnel. Captain James Tyrrell had the motor vessels the Tyrronell, the Halronell and the Murell. Captain Michael Tyrrell had the auxiliary motor schooner the JT and S and then the M.V. Avondale. Captain John Tyrrell had the auxiliary motor schooner the Invermore and then the M.V. Alfred Mason. Kevin Kearon had the motor vessels the Reginald Kearon, the Gloria, the George Emily and the Sea Bank. Victor Hall had the M.V. Kilbride and had shares in various schooners like the Venturer, the De Wadden, the Harvest King, the Happy Harry and the M.E. Johnton.

Chapter 4

M.V. Tyrronall

THE NEXT SHIP I joined was the M.V. Tyrronall and I was there from the 1st January 1955 until 31st December 1955, exactly one year, as ordinary seaman (OS), at the going rate of two pounds and ten shillings per week. The M.V. Tyrronall was built in Germany as the Helmat in 1935 as an auxiliary type three-masted Baltic schooner (199 GT[1], 99 NT[2], 107 feet by 23 feet by 8.9 feet). She was lengthened in 1939 to 136.6 feet, which increased her tonnage to 244 gross, 122 net and 330 deadweight. She was powered by a Deutsche Welke A.G. which gave her a speed of 7.5 knots.

In 1945 she was handed over to the Ministry of War Transport and was renamed Empire Contamer and was used in the coastal trade. She grounded near Fowey suffering bottom damage. Bought in that port by Jim Tyrrell of Arklow, she was repaired and renamed Tyrronall. Two masts were eventually removed and she had two derricks fitted on her main mast amidships and was fitted with two diesel powered winches.

When I joined her in 1955 she had no mod cons, and the only navigation aid was a portable direction-finder. Four men lived forward in the fo'c'sle and three aft in the poop. She had an unusual hatch arrangement in that the hatch boards went on twartships over fore and aft wooden beams which in turn rested on twartships lift-out steel beams. Putting these fore and afters in place was very risky as it had to be a co-ordinated, two-man job where both men had to walk

[1] GT: Gross Tonnage
[2] NT: Net Tonnage

out on the beams, one man on each and lift and swing each fore and after beam into its position in one smooth motion, otherwise one or both men were liable to be pulled off balance and fall down the hold. This happened to quite a few people over the years.

I stayed in the Tyrronall for one year, mostly trading between Dublin, Widnes and Haulbowline Island for Irish Steel. Haulbowline was the site of the Irish Steel, to whom we were chartered to. We lifted scrap in Dublin and coal in Widnes for their furnaces. The island was also the base of the Irish Navy. We would also take the odd run to Par, in Cornwall, and Ballinacur, in Cork harbour, to load china clay for the pottery in Arklow and to Clonakilty, Wicklow, Youghal, Belfast, Garston, Barry and Cardiff, carrying mainly coal to Ireland and pit props back to the U.K.

M.V. Tyrronall

CHAPTER 5

British Shipping Federation

MY NEXT SHIP was the Fremantle Star (ON[3] 169518), when I joined the British Shipping Federation, or the *Pool,* as it was widely known. I joined the ship in Liverpool on the 1st April 1956 and signed on the Blue Star ship the next day as ordinary seaman for a run job to Glasgow, where we discharged frozen meat and general cargo and back loaded general and the usual whisky for Australia and New Zealand. I was paid off in Liverpool on 13th April 1956.

Before leaving Dublin I had applied to sit for an Efficient Deck Hand (EDH) Certificate so I had to go back there to be examined.

In those days Blue Star Ships did not carry radar sets, it was said that one of their ships had been involved in a collision which had been radar-assisted, which resulted in all radar sets being removed from all their vessels. It was only in later years that it was decided to re-fit them again.

My next ship S.S. Ravenshoe (7295.32 GRT[4]), a war-built empire ship with coffin stern, owned by John Cory and Sons of Cardiff, built by Short Brothers in Sunderland 1945. She was a typical British tramp steamer, a 'tween decker with five hatches, number 1 and 2 on the fore deck, number 3 on main deck between bridge and stokehold and 4 and 5 on after deck. All hatches, 'tween and main deck, were fitted with hatch boards and tarpaulins. She had a raised fo'c'sle head. The bridge housed the officers' saloon, 1st, 2nd and 3rd mates' cabins on the main deck. On the 2nd deck containing the master's and radio

---

[3] ON: Official Number

[4] GRT: Gross Register Tonnage

officer's quarters and on the bridge deck there was the wheel house, chart room and radio shack. Over that was the monkey island. The galley and engineers' quarters, engine room and stokehold were abaft the number 3 hatch. The boat deck was on top of this accommodation, as was the cadets' quarters for four men.

Navigation equipment consisted of a radio direction finder, a Walker's patent trailing log and the navigation officers' skills, using the sun, moon, stars, planets and landmarks when available. There was no radar fitted and no air conditioning.

I signed on as EDH in Bidston Dock, Birkenhead, sailed for Vitoria, Brazil to load iron ore for Cardiff. I paid off here on 13th June 1956, the day my father died in an accident on board the M.V. Menapia in Drogheda. The ship's agent passed the news of his death to me and he was good enough to make all arrangements for me and my brother Billy, who happened to be in Barry loading coal in one of Munroe's Colliers, the Kyle Castle, to meet me and for both of us to travel home together. Needless to say, it was a sad return.

CHAPTER 6

Irish Shipping

THE S.S. IRISH Elm was my next ship, which I joined in Glasgow on 10th August 1956 and left on the 22nd June 1958 in Dublin. She was 5827.61 GT, 3208.93 NT, 400098 ON, 499 NHP[5], and carried four passengers.

She had five holds with 'tween decks and with deep tanks in the number 3 hold. She was also fitted with refrigerated cold rooms in the number 2 and 3 'tween decks and a tonnage hatch aft of the number 5 hold on the main deck. There was two derricks on each hold plus one jumbo derrick over number 2 hold. She had a raised fo'c'sle head with the 1 and 2 holds forward of the bridge, a long boat deck and housing amidships which held all the accommodation. Across the fore part, on the main deck, was the officers' and passengers' lounge and dining saloon, above that was the passengers' accommodation on the boat deck and above that the master's, chief engineer and radio officers' quarters while above that was the bridge, chartroom and radio shack. Abaft the saloon and lounge on the main deck was the galley and pantry amidships, the ratings' recreation room was amidships on the aft end. Along the port side was the engineers' cabins and aft of them was the petty officers cabins, bosun, lamp trimmer, carpenter, chief cook, 2nd cook, donkeyman and their mess room.

Along the starboard side from forward were the 1st, 2nd and 3rd officers, chief and 2nd steward's, deck crew's mess room, pantry, and engineer ratings' mess room, assistant stewards, cabin boy and

---

5 NHP : Nominal Horse Power

galley boy's cabins. On the boat deck from aft on the passengers' accommodation was the number 3 hatch. Galley and stokehold fidleys or skylights, then the funnel and engine room fidleys and abaft that there was house which accommodated four cadets, their study and bathroom.

The crew was accommodated in single rooms amidships below the main deck, the sailors on the port side and firemen and greasers on the starboard side. Accommodation was quite good, apart from the fact that the sailors' and engine ratings' cabins were situated right over the stokehold and engine room, and while this was not too bad in the cold North Atlantic, it was at times unbearable in the Tropics, where the bulkheads and deck became too hot to touch and the deck in the cabins too hot to walk on in bare feet.

One porthole in each cabin was the only cooling available, when you could open them. There was no air conditioning on the ship, only forced air sent down by fans and trunk ways, which, by the time it arrived down at the end of the line, was very poor indeed as it had lost most of the pressure. Opening the port hole in the lower cabins was fraught with danger as you could only open them on the lee side or if the weather was very calm. Many times you would fall asleep and get a dollop of water onto the bed if the ship altered course, the weather changed or even if you passed too close to another vessel's wash. If one cabin got flooded then all cabins suffered, as the water was free to run along the deck from one cabin to the next. The man living in the middle of the row of cabins came off the best, with minor flooding, when all the water ran forward or aft depending on the trim of the ship. In a major shipment of water all hands were flooded. A lot of our time was spent sleeping on number 4 hatch cover but this was never an option in the SW Monsoon.

Wooden slabs, which had to be handled by shore crane or ships derricks, covered the main deck holds. Hatch boards were used in the 'tween decks, tarpaulins covered all hatches, except when carrying grain cargoes when the 'tween deck tarpaulins were left off and feeders were constructed from the main deck coamings and hatch beams to the 'tween deck hatches. These feeders were put into place by the ships crew using heavy timbers, burlap and wooden laths, as were the shifting boards, which extended from below the feeders and 'tween deck hatches to almost half way down to the ceilings.

Fitting shifting and feeder boards, together with the heavy steel uprights necessary to hold the boards in position, was a very dangerous job indeed. It required working from bosun's chairs or stages rigged from the main deck hatch coamings, in almost all weathers, across the North Atlantic from the time of departure in Europe to the time of arrival in the loading port, which could be any place in North America from the Gulf of Mexico up the east coasts of United States, Newfoundland and Canada, including Ports in the St. Lawrence, the Great Lakes and Port Churchill in Hudson Bay.

In the province of New Brunswick, in which two regular ports of call for all Irish vessels were located, St. John and Dalhousie, there were most peculiar laws in force for the purchase and consumption of alcoholic beverages from the very few establishments in each port licensed to sell alcohol. These drinking dens opened at 6pm and closed at 10pm. No ladies were allowed in. There was no counter service, everyone sat at a table with four chairs at each table. Shifting table or chairs was not allowed. There was always a queue to get in, past the doorman who checked your I.D. before allocating you a seat.

In winter time it was invariably too cold to stand in the queue and you often missed your turn when you walked around the block to warm up. When you managed to get a seat it was often at a table with strangers as your shipmates would be settled at whatever chair was available at the time. Once at a table you were not allowed to change seats if another one became available. In fact, if you stood up, except to go to the toilet, you were promptly marched outside and, to get back in, you had to queue up again. Only one drink was allowed in front of each person and another would not be served until the glass was completely empty. These rules were rigidly enforced.

The Irish Elm was a very low powered-tramp steamer. I remember on one occasion being hove to in an Atlantic hurricane with the helm hard to port and the engine on full ahead for two days where she just managed to hold the seas on the port bow.

Most of the time was spent on the North Atlantic carrying general cargoes to and from North American to ports in Europe, the UK and Ireland. A typical cargo could include a general mixture of grain, rolls of news print, hogsheads of tobacco, raw hides, logs, sawn timber and meat eastbound. Westbound would normally be of smaller tonnage parcels which could be Irish meat, Irish chocolate, scotch whisky, Irish Hospital Trust Sweepstake tickets, horses, mares and stallions, cattle, bulls and cows for breeding, steel and steel pipes, motor cars and household goods and sometimes passengers, in both directions. On one trip we carried a variety of circus animals with their attendants, food and road transport.

On one particular voyage we left Cork on 22nd December 1956 and arrived back in Dublin on 6th December 1957 which took us to Norfolk, Virginia to load grain for Avonmouth, then to New Orleans to load soya beans for Shimazu and Kobe in Japan. That was a six-week trip via the Panama Canal, with a call at Hawaii for bunker oil. There were very poor port conditions at Shimazu, where they had not yet recovered fully from the war, which meant that we had to discharge out in the roads, into barges using the ship's equipment. Due to weather and conditions ashore it took about three weeks to discharge half the cargo, about 3.500 tons, using local labour which was made up of men and women. Cargo nets, in which sheets of burlap were spread, were lowered into the holds, spread out on top of the soya beans onto which the dockers scooped the grain. The ship's winches lifted the net by the four corners, turning the net and the burlap into an open-topped bag which was lifted out of the hold and lowered over the side and into the barge where three corners of the net were unhooked. The winchman then lifted the net by the one corner which emptied the grain into the barge. When full the barge was then towed ashore to be discharged. The same system of discharging was used in Kobe, except that the grain was landed on to the quayside into carts which were pushed away by squads of men.

After about three weeks in Japan we went to Seattle to load maize for Vishakhapatnam and Calcutta in India. Our great circle course from Kobe to Seattle took us well north into the cooler climate south of the Aleutian Islands.

S.S. Irish Elm Discharging Soya beans in Shimazu in Japan.

We met lots of Arklow family friends in Seattle and had many a merry night ashore with them and, after five days loading two different types of grain, we departed for India. It took us forty five days of very pleasant steaming to reach Vishakhapatnam with one call to Balikpapan in Borneo for fuel, water and fresh vegetables.

On arrival at Vizagapatam we were instructed to anchor off until further notice. There were reports of a famine in India at the time with about fifty ships waiting in the anchorage to discharge. Most ships had their lifeboats down and regattas were held on Sundays between ships crews. Fishing and visiting other ships was also common. Landing ashore was not allowed but, as the anchorage was so far off, it was not practical. After forty days at anchor we eventually got the pilot on board and proceeded inwards. Due to congestion in the port when we did manage to get inside we were compelled to anchor and moor off a river bank. Long planks were hauled off and narrow gangways were put in place between the shore and the ship. There were five pairs of gangways altogether; one pair from each hatch.

The method of discharge was bagging. The grain was bagged in the hold, lifted out with the ship's gear, landed onto a platform on the side deck, built up from the hatch slabs. The bag was then placed on the shoulder of a native who trotted down the bouncing gangway and dropped it neatly in position in a wagon and hauled away by bullocks.

In fifteen days, and after having discharged about half the cargo, we were ordered to proceed up to the Hugely River and discharge the remaining cargo. Nothing ever went smoothly in India at that time and we spent another two weeks at anchor in the roads waiting in the mouth of the Ganges for a berth.

I shall never forget the conditions which we experienced in Calcutta in those days, with the poverty and the plight of the citizens and we were all glad to depart after a week discharging. We received orders to proceed to Mauritius in the Indian Ocean to load a full cargo of bulk sugar for St. John, New Brunswick, in Canada.

We called at Colombo in Ceylon, now Sri Lanka, to take on fuel, water and fresh vegetables and after two days there we carried on to Port Louis in Mauritius. Six weeks we spent there, anchored fore and aft loading brown sugar. The port anchor cable was broken at two shackles and the anchor and chain carried aft in a barge where the anchor was dropped from the barge and the end of the cable brought on board and secured over the stern. The starboard anchor held the ship forward.

The sugar was loaded in bags into a barge ashore; the barge was then towed out to the ship where the bags were lifted on to the hatch boards using the ship's gear and bled into the holds after which the bags were sent ashore again for refilling.

The island was very beautiful and very poor in those days and the countryside appeared to be one vast sugar plantation. We had a very pleasant time there, but it was dragged out for too long and money was of short supply and crew overtime was down to the minimum. French was spoken ashore. The Flying Angel ran the Seamen's Club which served ice cold German beer and the Padre organized football matches between other ships and the local orphanage and prison. He also arranged tours and swimming outings to the only safe beach on the north coast, the harbour was full of sharks so swimming there was out of the question.

There was a race course in the very centre of town, which was a great attraction.

The workers were mainly of Indian origin and very poor, while the wealth of the island was in the hands of the French. There was a vast difference between the rich and poor. White rum was half a crown a bottle, two and six in old money, or about 18 pence in punts.

From Mauritius we steamed around the Cape of Good Hope and called into Cape Town for bunker fuel, water and stores. Our next Port of call was St. Vincent in the Cape Verde Islands to top up with more fuel, fresh water and stores and where the crew carried out a brisk trade in empty oil drums and spare clothing, in exchange for souvenirs of various types. We all suffered dearly for having flogged our clothing in St. Vincent for it was not long after leaving the Islands that the weather began to get noticeably colder as it was winter in the North Atlantic and the east coast of Canada was under snow, and ice packed the harbour and the Bay of Fundy. Our first concern was to get ashore and purchase some warm clothing.

After discharging the sugar we were ordered around the coast and up the Saint Lawrence to load grain in Three Rivers and Montreal, and then it was down to Botwood in Newfoundland to load rolls of newsprint and hides, all for Dublin and Cork.

After a few more trips across the North Atlantic and back to Western Europe I paid off the Irish Elm in Dublin on 22nd June 1958 and joined the Irish Fern on 31st July 1958, in Barry.

M.V. Irish Heather sister of Irish Fern entering Leixoes

The Irish Fern was a much different type of vessel. She was built as a diesel powered collier in Dublin in the early 1950. Her particulars were G.T. 1113, N.T. 522, O.N. 400118, and I.H.P. 1000 with deadweight cargo of about 900 tons. She was a typical collier with a raised fo'c'sle head, two holds, No 1 hatch cover in a well deck forward of the bridge and was fitted with the early type of McGregor steel hatches. The bridge was amidships between the two holds over a watertight bulkhead, which divided the two holds. The bridge structure held the accommodation for the master and two mates and with a small galley and saloon. The engine room was aft, with the engineers' accommodation, saloon, galley and cook steward on the main deck and the crew below. There was a large crew which consisted of master and two mates, bosun, six seamen, chief, 2nd and 3rd engineers, cook steward, 2nd steward, galley boy and cabin boy.

She was engaged in a trade from ports in the Bristol Channel to Portugal with coal and steel cargoes from Newport, Port Talbot, Barry or Cardiff and back with pit props from Lisbon, Oporto, Leixoes or Huelva.

We had a few nasty trips across the Bay of Biscay rolling heavily with steel on the way south and losing some pit props on the way north. There were times when the helmsman was unable, or was ordered not to, go forward or aft over the deck cargo of pit props to relieve his mate, this meant that those amidships were marooned there for the duration.

There was a nice lucrative little trade being carried out by some of the crew. Brandy being the main business north bound and bicycle tyres, inner tubes and typewriters south.

I left the Irish Fern at Port Talbot on 12th December 1958 and joined the British Ship S.S. Baron Murray in Birkenhead on 13th February 1959.

CHAPTER 7

S.S. Baron Murray

THE S.S. BARON Murray, of Ardrossan (O.N. 166215, N.R.T. 4206.72, G.R.T. 7022.89, and N.H.P. 341) was a war-built British tramp, a Baron Line ship, owned by H. Hogarth and also known as Hungry Hogarts.

Why did I join such a notorious shipping company? Jobs were scarce in Ireland at that time and as I was out of work I decided to go back to British Shipping Federation.

At that time I always seemed to be in trouble with the Shipping Federation, or The Pool as we all called it. As a member of the Pool you were required to do your time on a vessel, take the leave which you had earned and when that leave had expired you were required to report back to the Federation for re-employment, and you were never to take a job on a foreign flagged ship.

I almost always overstayed my leave, particularly if the fishing was good, and when you overstayed your leave you were going to have to suffer for it. Sailing on an Irish flagged vessel was also considered to be breaching the rules of the Pool. To become established again I had to take almost the first job offered as a form of punishment. I was told that I was to stand by the Baron Murray until she departed and sailed from Birkenhead's Bidston Dock, in case there were any last minute desertions and to make myself available to do a pier head Jump if required.

That is how I found myself, at three o' clock on a miserable winter's morning in February 1959, sitting and waiting in a taxi with three others, a stand-by steward and fireman and an official from the

B.S.F. and ready to replace anyone who might jump ship. Such was the name that the Baron Line, or Hungry Hogarths as it was known, had that it was the policy of the Liverpool branch of the B.S.F. to always have extra hands standing by up to the time until the Baron boat was gone and clear.

I was assured that she was only going on a voyage for six weeks, to Casablanca to load phosphates for Newport News and grain back to the U.K. and although I was aware of the Baron Line's reputation, I believed them and I figured that I could put up with whatever they threw at me for the six weeks it would take.

I was very naive in those days; I also thought that the chances of my being called were very slim. Sure enough my heart sank when it was decided that I was to replace a jumper. I was rowed out to the ship, which was being held by two tugs, in the middle of the West Float Basin waiting for the lock to fill and the gate to open. It was cold, miserable, wet and very dark at three o'clock in the morning, when someone finally lowered a heaving line for my gear and a pilot ladder for me to climb. When I got on board I was told to get changed and lend a hand on deck.

After we finally cleared the lock gates the ship had to be battened down, derricks lowered, ropes stowed and watches set. I found that I was on the 8 to 12 watch which meant that I would not get off the deck until at least midday. After watch I was told to go along to the store room to be issued with my bedding, weekly supply of dry victuals, soap, knife, fork, spoon, mug and plates.

For breakfast that first morning, after having been up all the night and to set the pace for the rest of the voyage, we were informed that as the galley stove was out of order that we would receive two boiled eggs, two slices of bread and a slice of spam each. The eggs were boiled in the steam geyser in the crew mess; a large pot of tea also came out of the geyser. The oil fed drip tray type stove had a habit of failing, we suspected, at the whim of the chief steward or cook.

We never saw another egg for a week as we were held rigidly to the Board of Trade rations, and for which we signed on for, which entitled us to two eggs per week, one can of condensed milk, one ounce of tea or milk, half pound margarine and so on. The list of what I was entitled to and their substitutes was too long to remember. Dry stores such as milk, tea, sugar etc. had to be collected once per week from the steward and hoarded, but as there was no fridges available to us the butter or whatever soon turned to liquid in the Tropics. The condensed milk would keep if you punched two holes in the top of the can and plugged them immediately after use with two wooden plugs which you made for that purpose. We also had to sow a canvas bag of one gallon capacity with a small hole at the top for filling and pouring, and two rope handles for hanging under the awnings for the cooling effect of the wind and shade. This was the only water we received and which had to do us for a day for drinking, washing and dobhing. It was issued once per day by the mate and a cadet, from the one fresh water rotary pump, kept locked, which was outside on the galley bulkhead and on view from the Bridge.

The boilers were big consumers of fresh water, particularly if they and the rest of the machinery was badly maintained and fresh water had to be bought and paid for and also the less water you carried the more cargo you could load. The mate calculated the amount of oil, stores and water which would be consumed from one port to the next allowing a percentage, based on experience, for eventualities such as weather likely to be encountered or any other unforeseen delays which might occur; hence the reason for the water rationing.

During the 1950s and 60s we never worried to much about the state of the water. We hooked up to the water main when we were in port, if the mains came anywhere close to the vessel, and if it was not available from that source it was delivered by barge. Some of those water mains and barges had a lot to be desired and were not always hygienic. There were nearly always rats in and around the connections on shore and the barges were usually clapped out rusty hulks, with the barge crews sometimes observed washing in it while the water in the hull sloshed around gathering rust and spilling over the open hatch coamings on to the deck where the crew slept, ate, did their ablutions and spat beetle nut juice continuously. We often remarked about this and shouted to the barge crews to refrain, but other than that we drank the water and used it in the boilers, and only worried if we could not get enough of it. Tramp Steamers had no water making equipment on board in those days and bottled water was unheard of.

In the old sailing ship days water was transported out to a ship at anchor in the roads by cleaning out a ships boat, towing that boat ashore, loading as much water as possible into the boat and towing it back to the ship by a second boat where it was emptied by buckets into the water tank. This exercise was repeated until enough water was taken.

In the schooners, which had normally only one boat on board, the operation was somewhat different. The boat was used for all kinds of operations, such as painting over the side, running mooring ropes, loading stores and landing personnel so, when required to carry fresh water it was imperative that the boat was cleaned out. It was then lowered over the side with two oarsmen and a coxswain and rowed ashore where it was loaded with water and rowed back to the vessel with the crew sitting on the thwarts up to their backsides in water.

The Baron Murray was a typical British tramp of the time, raised fo'c'sle head, two holds on main deck forward of the bridge, number 3 hatch abaft the bridge housing which contained the master, sparky and deck officers. Aft of number 3 hatch was the galley which was the same width as the hatch coaming, with a door on each side, from which the boy or Peggy had to collect the cooked food in kits each meal time and carry it aft to the crew mess in all weathers. Abaft the galley was the stokehold, engine room and along each side was the engineers' cabins on one side and the petty officers' cabins on the other side. On top of this housing was the boat deck, funnel and a house which accommodated four cadets. Next number 2 and 5 holds, aft of them was the crew and firemen's mess rooms, toilets and wash rooms on the deck with the cabins which was made up of two, three and four berth cabins, depending on the shape of the hull around the stern, below the main deck. At the bottom of the access ladder to the crew's deck there was a door into the steering flat which, because of the noise from that, the propeller and the vibrations when the propeller lifted out of the water made sleep very difficult.

We had a mixed bag of men on board. The officers were nearly all Scots and the engineers were a mix of different nationalities. The Bosun was from Chile. The usual variety of Scots, Irish, Welsh,

English, Maltese and army dodgers were on deck, with Somali firemen and greasers below.

Before arrival in Casablanca we soon learned that, instead of loading for the States, we were now to load for Lorencho Marques in Mozambique, at that time Portuguese East Africa. As we had signed the normal two year agreement, this meant that we could be held to that and all the conditions it contained.

So we loaded a full cargo of phosphates rock in Casablanca and headed south for the Cape of Good Hope and up the South and East African Coast to Mozambique. Before we got there life on board had settled into a routine of bad grub, not enough water, and a daily deputation from the crew mess to the master or chief steward to complain about the food. We discovered too that there was to be the minimum of overtime to be earned. The watch on deck, the three day workers and the four cadets were all that were used to moor and unmoor, and as an AB's wage was only about thirty six pounds per month before stoppages, and overtime, one shilling and three pence per hour, you normally worked as many hours overtime as were available so that you had a few pounds to collect at the payoff and also the hours overtime helped to pass the time away and prevent boredom. So when you did your trick on the wheel you were then sent down to the main deck and joined the farmer of your watch to chip the main deck and rub waste oil onto the chipped deck before knocking off. It was the same routine day in and day out.

We made small awnings for ourselves to cover our backs from the burning sun as we bent and chipped the long hot main deck, a soul-destroying never-ending task. On completion of discharge of cargo at Lorencho Marques we were ordered down the coast to load coal in Beira for Mauritius. It was the dirtiest, dustiest coal I have ever loaded or even heard about. It got everywhere. For our own good we blocked and stuffed every vent, every opening and every entrance and then tried to eat and sleep in stifling conditions for two days, for there was no use washing down the ship, ourselves, our cabins or mess rooms until we had finished loading. There was a Union Castle liner, the Edinburgh Castle, moored close astern of us loading her general cargo and taking on passengers and she soon became covered with the dust before she moved off.

Finally we departed for Mauritius where we arrived in Port Louis in ten days and started discharging into barges from almost the same anchorage I was in before in the Irish Elm, and took almost as long to discharge the coal as it did to load the sugar, five weeks. I was able to renew my acquaintance with the Padre in the Seaman's Mission but this time the stay in Mauritius was not as pleasant as the previous one. There was a cloud over this ship, which had nothing to do with coal dust. There was very little money allowed to us. The rule, which was enforced by the master, was that after deductions from your basic pay such as allotment, tax, insurance and slop chest, you were only allowed a percentage of your remaining basic pay. We were not allowed to draw on our overtime earnings, even if we had some overtime.

From Mauritius we were ordered to Marmagoa in Goa which was then a Portuguese state on the west coast of India, to load a full cargo of iron ore for Japan. Loading was carried out by an army of natives, men and women, carrying saucer shaped baskets on their head up gangplanks and dumping the contents down the hatches. I have to say that I found the Portuguese overseers the hardest taskmasters I have ever come across. Portugal at that time was a dictatorship and the workers there at the time were very poorly paid and had to put up with a lot of hardships and abuse.

While I was running there on the Irish Fern to Lisbon and Leixoes even the nuns who used to come to the ships with five or six orphans to beg for anything they could get had to hand over more than half to the police and soldiers who manned numerous checkpoints. Then this same crowd of poorly fed soldiers was sent overseas, given a bit of authority, a whip and a gun, and put in charge of the natives who they treated like animals.

While discharging phosphates at Lorencho Marques and loading coal at Beira the native workers were never allowed up or out of the holds until their day's work was finished which was normally twelve hours. They were fed once a day at midday when a fifty gallon oil drum part filled with some kind of slops was lowered down to them and where they all tucked in using their hands. They had to go to the toilet wherever they could and they had to be quick about it.

It took ten days to load and then we were on our way to Yokahama to discharge. The trip was uneventful and we discharged our cargo in three days and received orders to proceed to Hong Kong. Although the Captain had been advised against proceeding through the Strait of Formosa, as China and Formosa, now Taiwan was on a war footing. At the time the communists and the nationalists were at war with Chiang Kai-shek who had declared Formosa a republic and taken refuge there. The commies on the Chinese mainland often lobbed a few heavy shells across the Strait just to let them know that they had not forgotten them.

So just before midnight on a black night as we steamed along nicely and peacefully we were surprised to be blinded by a very powerful search light and the sound of an American voice demanding "what ship where to" and then when informed, the American voice said "This is a US Warship, now get your limey ass out of here". We never saw that ship, only the searchlight, otherwise she was in total darkness and that was the days before radar was carried on all merchant ships and there was no VHF or medium range radio on board the Baron Murray. Hogarths never put anything on board their ships unless it was compulsory and they were required to do so by the Board of Trade.

On arrival in Hong Kong we anchored in the harbour to await further orders and a few days after we were told that we were dry docking in Kowloon. We docked late at night and were all secure in dock by daylight. There was a row of about six dry docks almost in a straight line next to each other along the waterfront on the Kowloon side of the harbour. The crew was split in two and half given shore leave and a sub[6]. I was among the first half of the crew to go ashore and we departed the ship mid morning to see the sights of Hong Kong.

When we arrived back in the dockyard in the dark that evening we could not find our ship. We walked up and down along the line of dry docks looking for the Baron Murray but she was nowhere to be found. Finally, we stood back and had a good hard look for anything that looked like her until we found one, but her name was different and her hull had a complete fresh coat of paint all over. We were not exactly sure until we got on deck and recognised fittings which were

---

[6] Sub: a cash advance on wages

familiar. In these days, before paint rollers, paint sprays and high pressure hoses, we found it remarkable that the hull could be cleaned off, scraped, washed, repainted, with the name and port of registry all changed in a matter of hours. She was now named "Cathay" and registered in Hong Kong. That same night the dock was flooded and the Cathay was moved out to anchor.

It never ceased to amaze me how the crew was never informed of anything and there always existed a big divide between officers and men. I always thought that it was the attitude of the company and the manner of the senior officers on board, who all seemed to have served their time in the company and had never experienced any other business or trade. It did not help either that the crew were always sending deputations to the bridge complaining about the food and the preparation of it, and quite rightly too.

The second and third officers, both of whom had served their time as cadets in the Baron Line, would have a fry-up in the chart room every night. The third mate would start the ball rolling at 2330 hrs when he would open up the iron rations and soon after the helmsman and the lookout on the bridge would start to get the smell of bacon and sausages. It was enough to drive us mad.

It took a lot of planning and experience to stock up for six months with cans of food such as sausages and other meats and perishables and a small portable one ring electric cooker, as apart from the main storage freezer which was kept under lock and key and carefully watched by the steward, there was no fridges in the mess rooms, galley or saloon. So whatever they purchased had to keep for a long time in all kinds of climates and there was no air conditioning either.

The second and third mates were typical of all the rest of the officers and engineers on board, in that all had their hoard of dry stores. They had all served their time well with Hungry Hogarth.

One day, after clearing the dockyard, we were told to pack our gear as we were being relieved the next day. We were then accommodated ashore in Hong Kong in the Seaman's Mission where we were placed in dormitories. The officers were sent elsewhere. We stopped there for two weeks waiting for transport back to the UK. We were given two pounds once a week by the agent, who gave us very little information as to what was planned for us, so we walked around the city all that time with little money and speculated as to what was going to happen to us, we figured that we were all going to be split up and sent home on different ships as Displaced British Seamen (DBS). We never had any contact with any of the officers since coming ashore and at times we felt very abandoned. At that time there was a large presence of Navy personnel in that part of the world, both British and American and they used Hong Kong for rest and recuperation. We spent a lot of time in the USA forces club which was named The Pacific Ocean Club and where all supplies were subsidised by the US Government.

Then one day the agent's runner informed us that we were to be ready to shift out the next day when a coach would collect us and deliver us to the airport and flown home. This was almost unheard of in 1959 and I think that not one of us had ever been up in a plane before, and so, at the airport we were reunited with our long lost officers and boarded what appeared to be a clapped out war-built Dakota or something similar. Some of our shipmates were very reluctant to board and had to be talked or cajoled into stepping on and so we set out for Singapore. On arrival in Singapore we remained on board and were relocated seats. Some time later an Italian crew boarded and took up the empty seats.

Our Somali black gang was given seats in the back of the plane, the Italians were seated in seats ahead of them, and our crew was seated ahead of the Italians and all the officers ahead of us in the front. We eventually set off, next stop Calcutta where we arrived late that same evening, but not without incident.

About halfway through the flight a fight broke out in the after end of the plane between the Somalis and Italians and this spread forward with some people running away from the fight and others chasing them. This shift of weight altered the balance of the plane as she took a bit of a nose dive, which frightened the heart out of all hands, including the flight crew and was enough to get everyone back into their seats. But it did not stop the bickering in the back.

It turned out that the Somalis all came from Italian Somalia Land, a colony which was lost to the Italians when they lost the war. It seems that there was no love lost between the Italians and the Somalis.

On arrival in Calcutta we were installed in the Great Eastern Hotel where we were given a meal and a room in the basement, but no money, which annoyed us but not as much as it annoyed the hotel lackeys. We strolled through the hotel looking through glass panels at the British Raj in their evening dress, male and female, all doing their Raj thing, having dinner, drinking and dancing the night away.

The poor old Indian servants and waiters were very disappointed with us because we were not able to tip them or give them buckshee, and they let us know it, particularly the next morning when we were leaving and when we left no food behind. We cleared the breakfast table and our rooms of all eatables and drinks as we knew from the previous day that we would get nothing until our arrival at the next port of call.

We boarded the same plane with the same crew early where we found that the seating arrangement had been adjusted and the British crew was seated between the Italians and the Somalis.

There was a short stop at Bombay where we refuelled and had a meal. Then we took off for Famagusta in Cyprus where we spent another night in a hotel. The next morning we took off, with the same craft, crew and seating arrangements for Milan, where we dropped off the Italians. With a full load of fuel we went direct to Southend, on the Thames estuary, and were coached into London where we were given and signed for two pounds 'Channel Money', which meant that officially we were now off pay from that moment, and as it happened that it was a Friday night we could not sign off and collect our balance of wages until the Mercantile Marine Office opened on Monday.

This meant that we had to find our own accommodation and food for two days, all on two pounds.

In all, I was five months on articles and I collected twenty one pounds including twenty six shillings in overtime when I finally signed off. One final humiliation occurred while travelling in from the airport when the luggage door in the back of the coach burst open and spewed most of the baggage all over the road, which, by the time we stopped and collected it some of it was damaged and bags were burst and run over by following traffic. We never did get compensation.

The following song was well-known in the British Merchant Navy at the time.

THE BARON LINE SONG

(Chorus) . . . . Roll along you hungry bastards roll along.
To Basra, Hong Kong, Rio or Chittagong
"Ropey Ropners" may be fine,
But give me the Baron Line,
Roll along you hungry bastards roll along.

CHAPTER 8

S.S Esso Westminster

WHEN I NEXT reported in at the Shipping Federation in Liverpool
they sent me down to Fawley in Southampton Waters to join my next
ship on the 23rd September 1959. She was the S.S Esso Westminster
(O.N 186019, G.T.17540, N.T. 10247, and S.H.P. 13750) and at that
time she was one of the largest ships in the world at 64,000 tons
deadweight. I thought at the time that ships could not get any bigger
than this, but I was very much mistaken. This was the start of things
to come, from then onwards tanker tonnage escalated.

The bridge was midships, with the deck officers', radio officers'
and owners' accommodation. The rest of the crew was housed in the
poop as was the officers' saloon and smoke room, the crew recreation
room and mess room. Each crew member had his own single room,
which was massive, as was the rest of the accommodation. It was as
if the builders did not know what to do with all the space available
to them.

The grub was first class with no restrictions and food was
available in the mess any time you wanted. She was built with a fair
size swimming pool on the boat deck and for the first time in my
life I found myself shipmates with an air conditioning system. What
a culture shock after Hungry Hogarth's Baron Line! I think that air
conditioning was one of the best things that ever happened on ships.
It enabled all hands to get a good night's sleep no matter where your
cabin was situated on the ship. There was no more tossing and turning
drenched in sweat in a cabin where you could not open a porthole
and no more dragging your bed out on deck for an hour before

getting yourself and your mattress soaked in a Tropical downpour. It also enabled you to enjoy the meals and relax better in the cooled atmosphere. Everything about her was on a vast scale and, compared to what I had been used to, she was a palace.

It was the practice in those days on tankers for the crew members who worked down the cargo tanks, cleaning, removing scale or wax, repairing valves or pipelines, to receive a large tot of rum when they returned to deck. This was issued to each man by the chief officer who stood by the hatch entrance with a large bottle of Four Bells Rum. As each man stepped out on deck he received a large tot and he had to be seen to drink it on the spot. This was to prevent him passing it on to another or taking it away to his cabin.

I joined and left her at the Esso Oil refinery in Fawley, which is just inside Calshot Point in Southampton Waters and made two round trips on her to Caripito in Lake Maracaibo, Venezuela, to load a full cargo of Crude oil each trip. Both trips were uneventful but I do remember that, as there were no tugs, to swing the ship onto the berth at Caripito it was necessary to drive her bow into the soft bank of the jungle and swing her on the rudder and propeller. The forecastle head had to be cleared of all hands during this operation as it was never known what might drop out of the trees onto the deck. Maracaibo is the largest Lake in South America and has an outlet to the sea.

CHAPTER 9

Fishing Vessel Ros Liath

MY NEXT SHIP was somewhat smaller and, after spending some time at home for the Christmas of 1959, I joined the crew of the Fishing Vessel Ros Liath to chance my luck at the rich herring fishing based in Dunmore East and fishing in the Baginbun Bay, east of the Hook Head. We did not do well at that fishing because fishing methods had changed and the boat was too underpowered to keep up with the rest of the fleet. After six weeks of trying, the Skipper, Shamey Tancred, decided he had had enough. It was soul destroying watching other boats come in, heavily laden with herring, to discharge their loads and going out again to load more.

Boats and fishing had advanced rapidly in the previous few years, with boats becoming bigger, more powerful, with better technology, and different, heavier fishing gear. Gone were the days when fishing for herring involved casting a long train of drift nets over the side in waters with the experienced men observing the signs of herrings on the water. The signs to watch out for were seagulls and gannets sitting on the water and a sheen of oil floating on the surface amongst the sea birds. The oil indicated that herring under the surface were exuding oils which floated to the top and the birds were waiting for the fish to rise towards the surface when the sun went down below the horizon, as herrings were known to do.

In this new method of fishing the boats steamed around the sea at full speed, not looking for signs on the surface of the water, but looking into electronic machines which could show up large lumps of herring underneath. When they got a 'sighting' they turned fast and shot the net as quickly as possible before the shoal moved off. With luck and good judgement on the part of the skipper they could hit the shoal spot on and possibly fill the boat with that one shot.

The problem was, in the spawning grounds in the Baginbun Bay, the herring shoals always seemed to travel close together in a not very large area. With up to maybe fifty boats racing around looking for them it could get quite hectic. Maybe three or four or even more boats might detect the shoals at the same time and shoot at the same time and then it could become quite dangerous. The boats worked in such close quarters of each other that fouling each other's gear was quite common and unintentional ramming sometimes occurred. It became a game of survival of the fittest and who dared won.

We were in the smaller and less powerful boats and stood no chance. But I would not have missed it for the world and by catching less fish we had more time off and more time to enjoy ourselves.

Fishing for the same shoals of herring were the Scotch Ringers, so named because that type of fishing originated in Scotland. They used a purse net and fished at night in pairs when the herring left the bottom. They also steamed around looking for a 'trace' on their echo sounders and when they found a shoal one boat shot the net in a ring around the herrings while the other boat picked up the end from the water, then the two boats pulled an end each and steamed ahead and closed each other until they came alongside. They now had the shoal trapped inside the ringnet. The next step was to close the bottom of the net so that the fish could not escape. To do this the two ends were passed on board one of the boats and the bottom rope was then pulled tight to close off the bottom of the net forming a large purse from which the herring could not escape. That is unless there was a tear in the net which happened for various reasons. The net was made of very fine twine and was fine-meshed, this was because the net covered a large area and stowage space on deck was restricted, so the net was made out of fine twine so as to not take up too much bulk on deck. It was often torn when being shot if the net had not been stowed properly prior to shooting it, as it ran out at speed and any little snag could cause a rip through layers of stowed netting.

While the first boat pulled on board more and more net and compacting the fish trapped in it, most of the second boat's crew jumped on board the first to help recover the fish. If they did not get enough herring in that one shot then they reversed the roles and went for another shot, the crew all transferring back to their own vessel. With the amount of herring congregating in the Baginbun Bay to spawn and the demand of the buyers to purchase it, it was like the Klondike, with Dutch, Belgium and Polish luggers waiting to load the catches.

All fishing boats had to go back to Dunmore East where the catches were auctioned, after producing a sample of your catch to the auctioneer for inspection by the buyers. The buyers would then send you off to a berth or to any one of the luggers anchored off the port. There, the herrings would be salted and barrelled and loaded on board for shipping out.

But it could not last, just as other herring grounds around our coasts did not last.

It was shamefully allowed to be exploited by governments and fishermen, as were other fisheries and as they are still now, in 2008.

What really put an end to the herring fishery in the Baginbun was a rule brought out after Ireland joined the EU. This rule allowed only a certain amount of herring tonnage to be landed at Dunmore but it did not place a restriction on the amount of boats allowed to fish. When the quota was reached in Dunmore the remainder of the fish on the other boats was sprayed with a red dye and pronounced unfit for sale and then dumped at sea, after they were paid the going rate for the catch. The next day and all the following days' boats were allowed to do this all over again until the season finished.

Then there was the fishing of herrings for their roe. When the net, filled with fish, was hauled up to the boat's side, a sample of about a basket full was taken out of it for inspection, if a certain percentage of the sampled fish were without roe the catch was released and the boat continued to fish until the sample showed the right percentage of roe. All the fish released in this manner were drowned. This had to be one of the worst rules ever made by the EU and enforced by the Irish government and which ensured the devastation of the herring fishery. They still fish in the Baginbun for herring but only on a strict quota basis.

C H A P T E R **10**

Back to the Merchant Navy

WHILE AT HOME, broke after the disastrous fishing trip, I was offered a job as Mate on a locally-managed coaster. At that time no certificates were required in the Home Trade vessels, except on ships that carried passengers. The Home Trade waters were defined as being the waters around the British Isles and the near continent between Brest and the River Elbe.

The coaster was the Swedish-built MV Stella Mary (O.N.184826), registered in Stockton-on-Tees when I joined her and then re-registered in Dublin (O.N. 400254) on 30th March 1960. She was of 359.51 N.R.T. and about 800 tons deadweight. Purchased by Cement Roadstone Ltd, she was engaged in shipping stone from Drogheda to London, burnt ore from London to Rotterdam and coal from Rotterdam to ports in Ireland. Built as a foreign-going vessel by the Swedes with one hold and hatch to carry loose sawn timber from the Baltic, she was purchased by a firm in Stockton and then sold on to Roadstone.

She was a fine sea boat but it was very hard to hold on to deck crews. The hatch coamings were 1.6 meters high and with heavier than normal double hatch boards it took three men to lift one from the side decks to the top of the coamings. With only three deck hands carried, battening down took too long to carry out.

The layout of the cargo hold was not suitable for bulk cargo discharge by grabs, which caused a lot of damage to the structure. She was a bad buy for Roadstone who quickly sold her on. I joined her at Drogheda on 8th March and left her in Drogheda on 4th May 1960.

            49

I then went back to the British Shipping Federation where I was sent to Manchester to join the S.S. Manchester Merchant (O.N.182613, GT7651.33, NT4594.89). We went with general cargo, motor cars and twelve passengers to Montreal, where we discharged all cargo and passengers. We then loaded grain and general for the return trip to Manchester and took on another twelve passengers for the return trip east. On the way we called at Botwood, in Newfoundland, for rolls of newspaper all for discharge at Manchester.

Traversing up and down the Manchester Ship Canal was a bit of a work in a big ship like the Merchant which was near enough the maximum size of vessel able to safely transit the canal, with the help of two tugs, at that particular time in 1960. It was a slow process, first you had to berth at Eastham Locks at the entrance to the canal to lower the topmasts and lift off the top section of the funnel so that the ship could get under the bridges. Then the tug boats hooked on again and began to manoeuvre the ship towards Manchester, which would at least take twelve hours, depending if you got a clear run and there were no snags. There were four systems of locks to negotiate and if there was another ship outward-bound she had priority so that the inward-bound vessel was obliged to hold back close to the lock to let the other vessel out. There were lay-by berths at intervals along the canal for vessels to tie up and allow others to pass, and also for emergencies. As this was the age before VHF all ships received their orders verbally from the Lock Master as you passed through each lock.

On arrival at Manchester the crew were paid off and offered a standby job on board while the ship was loading and discharging. But we were not allowed to live on board, as that was company policy, which was good for local seamen but was not satisfactory for us as we would have had to find accommodation ashore. So I paid off the Manchester Merchant in Manchester on 21st June 1960. I met my future wife while I was home on leave and this was to change my whole way of life.

There was a seaman's strike in the U.K. at the time and my next ship was the M.V. Irish Fir, which I joined in Cork on 4th July and left in Manchester on 18th August 1960 (O.N. 400176, G.T. 1751, N.T. 742, N.H.P. 303 and D.W. 1200.) Her large gross tonnage was attributed to the large accommodation block to house a very large crew for a vessel of her size. The crew was made up of the Master, three deck officers, a radio officer, one bosun, six deck crew, four engineers, two greasers, two stewards, two cooks and two cabin boys; a total of twenty four men, a big crew for such a small ship.

We loaded steel pipes in Manchester for Halifax and rolled our way across the Atlantic suffering from the effects of a heavy swell left from the aftermath of hurricanes to the south.

We then steamed around the coast to load loose timber back for Manchester. While crossing the Atlantic the deck cargo of timber had to be checked and lashings tightened every day because the heavy swell and the rolling of the ship caused the timber to move and loosen the lashings. Timber carrying ships which carried deck cargoes invariably arrived at their discharge ports with a list to one side or another. This was caused by the consumption of fuel and fresh water in the course of the voyage, both of which were carried and stowed in the lowest part of the ship. At the same time the sawn deck cargo of timber soaked up a certain amount of water caused by rainfall and spray. The reduction of weight in the lower part of the ship and the increase of weight in the deck cargo higher up caused the ship's centre of gravity to move upwards and altered the vessels stability. This raising of the centre of gravity was well-known and was allowed for in the mate's calculations prior to loading. However, what could not be calculated were delays which might occur during the loaded voyage to the discharge port which might be caused by bad weather or engine trouble.

Very often vessels arrived or entered ports of refuge with severe lists and often the deck cargo had to be jettisoned to lower the centre again to bring the ship back to positive stability. Special timber lashings which secured the deck cargo were fitted with special slip turnbuckles to enable the crew to carry out this procedure. It could be a very dangerous job as the crew member had to be on top of the cargo with a mallet and when the slip was made there was always the danger that he might be carried overboard with the timber. The timber arrived alongside in already-slung bundles and measured in standards. It was then lifted on board by the ships gear and each plank was handled and stowed individually by the dockers or longshoremen just like a giant jigsaw puzzle.

As the planks arrived at the ship in different lengths, width and thickness it was the only way to stow the cargo to get the maximum tonnage or standards on board. Discharging the timber was even more difficult than stowing it as the dockers had to pick it from under their feet, place it in bundles of the same dimensions and sling it for lifting out by crane. They could not dig down as each layer was knitted in and could only be taken from the top.

This was the days before timber was parcelled and stowed in units with all planks of the same dimensions and weighing about five tons each, ready for transporting, slinging and stowing with fork lifts. In those days, the holds of the ships were shaped by the hull so as to take the maximum amount of cargo using the maximum amount of space available. Nowadays the holds are all squared off under large hatch openings to facilitate the fast discharge and loading of palletized and containerized cargoes with the minimum of labour. Older ships holds were larger, space-wise, to accommodate a lot of broken stowage due to general cargo arriving in easier handled lots.

My next ship the S.S. Runa, one of Glens of Glasgow (ON 180848, GT 1942, NT 963). She was discharging loose timber in Dublin. We went around to Newcastle on the Tyne to load coke for Stockholm. Coke, being light, soon filled up the cargo hold. Then a large cage was constructed of timber frame and chicken wire around the decks to take the deck cargo. With the coke deck cargo we lost sight of the main deck or the hatches again until it was discharged. On the passage to the Baltic we were able to step off the boat deck, climb over the heaps of coke to get to the fo'c'sle head or to the poop.

Coke is the remains of coal when the gas is extracted out of it in the gas works and it is then used in steel smelters for the intense heat it is able to generate. It is not a very nice cargo to load as it is very porous and soaks up water which is liable to make the deck cargo top heavy and could cause the ship to lose stability. The deck is also very difficult to negotiate in the dark when relieving the wheel and the lookout. The dust blows off it and being very gritty it was very hard on the eyes, and we were never clean. The coke was discharged and then we went around the coast to a saw mill and loaded a full cargo of processed timber, below and on deck, for discharge in Glasgow.

I left her in Glasgow on 24th November 1960 as I was setting myself up to attend the Nautical College when it re-opened after the Christmas recess.

Glasgow steamer "Runa" at Preston, '50   R S Collection

Runa

My next ship was the M.T Caltex Whitegate, later renamed Texaco Whitegate (P.O.R. London, O.N.300968, G.T. 2022.34, N.T. 1110.78, S.H.P.1640). I joined her on 30th November and left her in dry-dock in Birkenhead on 16th January 1961. She was engaged in carrying refined produce from Whitegate oil refinery in Cork Harbour to Dublin and Limerick. Previously she was one of what was known as the Mosquito Fleet, built for trading in and around Lake Maracaibo. She was twin screw with bridge amidships. The accommodation was very bad as she had been built as a day boat for her work in the Caribbean and the crew accommodation was added when she was transferred to work in European waters.

On leaving the Caltex Whitegate, I attended, as arranged, the Irish Nautical College which was situated on the shore end of the West Pier in Dun Laoghaire. There were two teachers in the College at that time, Captain Tom Walsh and Mr. Ken Dixon.

When I began to study for a Certificate of Competency as a deck officer I thought only of a Mate Home Trade but as there was a certain amount of overlap in a Home Trade and a 2nd Mate's Foreign Certificate I found, while studying on my own and mostly in secret on board ships, I had gone deeper into the syllabus of the Foreign Certificate than intended. There was only one thing bugging me, mathematics. I had never advanced very far in that subject at primary school as they only taught very basic sums but I remember being always interested in that subject. One day, when I was in Baltimore, Maryland loading grain on the Irish Elm I bought a book called 'Mathematics Made Simple', which I still have. If it was being published now it would probably be labelled 'Mathematics for Dummies'. A marvellous soft back, it started off at the very beginning at one and one are two, two and two are four etc. and went right through to algebra and trigonometry.

I explained my situation to Capt. Tom Walsh, the Principle of the Nautical College and after a short verbal examination he advised to go for the Foreign Certificate. I sat for my second Mate's Certificate in The Mercantile Marine Office, Eden Quay, Dublin in April 1961 and after one failed attempt I sat again the next month and passed on the 16th May. I then went on to join the British and Irish Steam Packet Company on 20th May.

CHAPTER 11

British and Irish Steam Packet Company

As I was short of cash I took a temporary job to earn enough money to buy a uniform and a sextant so that I would then be able to sail on foreign-going vessels. I joined the British and Irish Steamship Company Ltd., Dublin. This was a cross-channel company that traded between Ireland and England and had cattle boats, general cargo and passenger vessels.

My first ship was the M.V. Kilkenny (O.N. 159736, and P.O.R. Dublin). She was engaged in the livestock trade from Dublin to the lairage in Birkenhead and general cargo and cars for Prince's Dock in Liverpool.

Next I was sent to their M.V. Inniscarra (O.N. 400016, N.T.280.3), which was a smaller general cargo vessel and traded from the Irish ports of Dublin, Drogheda, Dundalk and Newry to Liverpool and Preston.

Then I joined the M.V. Dundalk (O.N. 159826, N.T, 272.56) which was a general cargo and cattle boat. We loaded livestock in any one of the above-named Irish ports for discharging at Birkenhead and general cargo for Liverpool with general cargo for the return trip from Liverpool.

Then when I was able to purchase a uniform I was promoted to the passenger and cattle boat the M.V. Leinster (O.N.159877, G.T.4144.85). In Dublin we loaded general cargo, cattle and passengers, in that order. We departed Dublin at 2000 hours every second day except Sunday and arrived at Birkenhead at about 0500 hours the next morning when we offloaded the cattle. We then shifted across the Mersey into the Prince's Dock where the passengers were disembarked and the cargo discharged. We then loaded the return cargo and passengers for Dublin and departed Prince's at 2100 hours, to arrive Dublin at 0700 hours.

Our sister ship, the M.V. Munster ran opposite us and as we both carried mail we never missed a sailing, regardless of the weather. This was also the days before containers and ro-ro and everything had to be lifted on and off, including cars. With the exception of the cattle of course, which were run on and off through doors in the ship's side and down cattle gangways into the lairage.

At times the poor cattle used to suffer horrible abuses at the hands of the cattlemen when loading and discharging and were beaten and prodded with electric cattle-prodders to keep them moving.

During the busy Christmas and summer holiday seasons the cattle pens in the aft section of the 'tween deck would be cleared out to make room for the increase in passenger traffic. Wooden bulkheads would be erected in place to separate the passengers and the cattle who shared the same deck. The space would then be hosed down, disinfected and hard wooden benches but in place for the doubtful comfort of the second class passengers.

M.V. Leinster

On deck, the number three cargo hatch, which divided the first and second class passengers, would be covered over and battened down, benches put in place to accommodate more people, and a canvas tent erected over the space to protect them from the elements. No amount of preparations could ever remove the smell or the sound of the cattle which could be heard mooing the other side of the partition. The ship was divided into first and second class accommodation, with the first class carried in the midship section and the second class in the poop. The second class occupied about one tenth of the total passenger space and held about six times more people. There were often not enough seats and people had to sit or lie down where they could. The smell alone could make you ill, and bad weather would aggravate the situation. After the eight hour trip across the Irish Sea some of the passengers were often put ashore in a pathetic state and it used to remind me of what conditions must have been like for the early immigrants.

At this early stage flying was just starting to take off and cross-channel passenger service was still a very lucrative business and a necessity. So, after I managed to buy a second-hand sextant in Dublin, I was getting quite dizzy racing back and forth across the Irish Sea, I declined their offer of a permanent job and decided to broaden my horizons, so I joined Irish Shipping as Third Officer, foreign-going.

CHAPTER 12

Back to Irish Shipping

ON THE 2ND February 1962, I was sent to join the M.V. Irish Larch (O.N. 400093, GT 6217.52, NT 3302.12, NHP 980) in Liverpool, as third officer. She was on charter to Cunard Line and when I joined in Liverpool she was discharging general cargo from the Gulf Ports in the USA and loading general for the return voyage.

A five-hatch job with 'tween decks and bridge amidships, she was loading and discharging at the same time and as this was the days before containers all cargo was wheeled out of the warehouse, slung on the dockside, lifted and lowered into the lower hold and stowed by hand. Cargo included almost everything in all shapes and sizes, in wooden crates, cardboard boxes and loose. Some cars were stowed in the 'tween deck.

Then we went to Glasgow to load more general and 2500 tons of whisky in the 'tween decks. This was a very sobering experience. I was put in charge of the four cadets and under the supervision of the chief officer, to tally and supervise the loading and stowage of the crates and cartons and to record everything including breakages. We also had to guard the Liverpool loaded cargo, some of which the Dockers could get at.

As regards the whisky, the dockers, hatch man and crane drivers had it off to a fine art. All the workers at that time carried billycans which contained their tea or other drinks. With the stevedores in position in the holds, they could not all be seen by the crane driver. The crane man was depending on the hatch man for directions and guidance as to where and when to land the pallet, which was loaded with up to sixty cases of whisky and sometimes more as the stuff came in full bottles, half bottles, nagins and baby bottles, all in different sized crates and cartons.

There were many accidents; cartons were damaged and bottles broken. Some were pure accidents and some were arranged accidents. This is where the billycans came into play. They were ideal for collecting spilled whisky from broken bottles as it leaked out of damaged cartons before they stowed the carton into position in the holds. As the crane lowered the pallet into the hatch it came under the control of the hatch man and at a signal from the dockers below the hatch man would guide the crane driver in such a way that the corner of the pallet would land on an obstruction which would tilt the load and cause one or more cartons to fall off, just high enough to break an odd bottle, without wrecking the carton. The carton would then be stowed and tallied, but not before all had filled their billycans, without noting the damage. By the end of the day some of the dockers would be unable to climb the ladders out of the hatches and they would have to be lifted out on the empty pallets by the crane and landed ashore. This was not at all unusual with this type of cargo. Some of our own crew was just as bad and there was whisky available for those who wanted it for the round trip to the gulf ports and back to the UK.

Discharging in the States was just as bad. Our first port of call in the Gulf Ports was Panama City in Florida, then to Houston, Galveston, New Orleans, Port Sulphur in the Mississippi and then to Baton Rouge. We discharged and loaded cargo in all these ports with parcels of whisky for all ports except Port Sulphur. Security was a nightmare as all cargo worked in these ports had to be accessed while working in holds containing whisky and everywhere we went the Longshoremen got some of it, but not so much as the Glaswegians as they had it down to a fine art.

One notable feature of these southern ports was that the black and white longshoremen never mixed even when they worked the same ship. When the whites worked the foredeck holds the blacks worked the aft deck, and vice versa.

We loaded bulk sulphur in Port Sulphur in two holds down through the 'tween decks which still held whisky for the next port. This was loaded via a chute from a gantry overhead, much like grain, which created a great amount of dust and it often burst into smouldering fire. This was attended to by directing the loading flow on to the fire and smothering it. Meanwhile, while loading, security watches had to be maintained to watch the whisky and to keep a fire watch. This meant that we had to stand in the dust all the time and we suffered. For three days afterwards the four of us who had kept the watch were blinded by the sulphur. We were never issued with any type of protection or told of the risk involved. However after some medical attention on board, administered by the chief steward, we recovered fully.

I do not know how much the insurance people were prepared to write off against loss and damages for the difference between the cargo loaded and that discharged but it must have been quite substantial. The losses we incurred seemed to be the norm in those days before containerization as we never heard any more about it.

The person I was relieving came back when we arrived in Garston and I was transferred to the M.V.Irish Fir (O.N. 400176, GT. 1751, NT.742, NHP 303), which I had previously served on as AB. She was still engaged on the North Atlantic from the U.K. to small ports in Canada, such as Parsborough, Campbell ton, Chatham, Rimouski and others.

Then we were sent to Fowey to load china clay for Genoa. This we were very glad of, as the year was going in and the hurricane season was approaching and we already had some dirty passages across the Atlantic. It was a nice change to be in the Mediterranean and after discharging in Genoa we went down to Nemours in Algeria with orders to load esparto grass.

Unfortunately, on arrival at Nemours there was a war going on. The locals were about to kick the French colonists out of the country. This was September 1962, and we had to wait at anchor for a few days for things to sort themselves out. We finally got word that it was safe to come alongside and load. As things were still a little confused the captain was uncertain as to what courtesy flag the ship should fly, so he decided to go in without putting any up. As soon as we tied up an armoured car approached the vessel and pointed a gun at the bridge and asked the captain if he wanted to buy a flag, which naturally he did. They charged the equivalent of one hundred pounds for it.

We left Nemours looking like a floating hay stack with the esparto grass piled high on deck for Watchet on the south coast of the Bristol

Channel, where, I believe it was to be used in the manufacture of high quality paper such as money. It looked more like straw rather than grass. The esparto grass was loaded in rectangular bales and the deck cargo was lashed, with difficulty, by using the ships timber lashings. The port and starboard vertical sides of the deck cargo was draped with old tarpaulins to prevent some of the spray from being soaked up by the grass and therefore upsetting the vessels stability. The top of the cargo was not covered and when the ship rolled, gaps would open and close in the top of the cargo.

On one occasion during an inspection of the cargo one of the crew disappeared down one of the gaps which kept opening and closing on him. He was fortunate in that he had been seen and we managed to get him out after a bit of a struggle.

I signed off the Irish Fir in Watchet on 1st Oct 1962 and went home on leave. On the 3rd December I joined the M.V. Irish Sycamore (ON 400296. GT 10560, NT 5740, BHP[7] 6800). I joined her in Avonmouth, where she was discharging grain, and from there we went to Belfast for a quick dry-dock, a hair cut and shave. We then loaded steel in Port Talbot for Durban and then went down the coast to Port Elizabeth to load iron ore for Bremen, where I left as the ship was going on a long-term charter and I had arranged to get married in June of that year. Four days later I joined my next ship.

I was transferred to the S.S. Irish Poplar (O.N. 400072, GT 8012.39, NT 4575.64, NHP 1107) which was engaged on the north Atlantic run, trading from Ireland and UK to east coast ports in the US from New York to Virginia. Back to general cargo and shifting boards again as most of the cargo was grain. We also loaded rolls of newspaper and hogsheads of tobacco in the 'tween decks.

I was three months on the Irish Poplar, leaving her on the 6th June and getting married on 10th June 1963. I had also arranged with Irish Shipping for me to attend the Irish Nautical College when it re-opened after the summer holidays. We spent our honeymoon in Scotland, mostly in and around Loch Lomond and enjoyed some runs up and down the lock on the passenger vessel the MV Maid of The Loch.

Prior to attending the college and during the school holidays I took a relief job as Master on the small coaster the MV Jackonia. She

---

[7] BHP : Brake Horsepower

had been owned by Wharton's of Goole and was purchased by a Mr. Nolan of Dublin who soon afterwards changed her name to Iveragh and re-registered her in Dublin. While I was there she was engaged in trading around the Irish Coast to ports like Cork, Newross, Wicklow, Drogheda and Derry, with cargoes of phosphates and grain. I was there for three weeks, relieving the Master and I took this opportunity to take my wife along for the period.

The cook left us during the period and my wife together with the chief engineer's wife, who was also on board, agreed take over the galley and share the cooking and the money. This was one of the coasters with no night generator. When cargo work was finished for the day and when there was no requirement to supply power to the electric winches or deck flood lights to assist the dockers the generator was shut down. This meant that the ship was then on oil lamps only. Seamen called them Bulkhead Generators and they gave off very poor light. Needless to say, they were also highly dangerous and needed to be treated with respect.

But they were never always treated with respect. They were often forgotten to be topped up with oil, or the wick was not trimmed, or the glass was not cleaned and all this would only be discovered or remembered when the crew returned back on board late at night in port, in the dark with only a match to light the way. This method of lighting was common on most coasters at the time and it encouraged men to get off the ship as there was never enough light to read by and everything was so quiet, with all the engines shut down, that you could hear every sound in the steel shell in which you were enclosed that it was almost impossible to sleep.

While at sea electricity was supplied by the shaft generator. This worked only off the main engine and while the propeller shaft was turning, it was originally only required to supply power to the navigation lights and selected accommodation lights while at sea.

In the following years, the Decca Navigation System was added to the load and that was followed soon after by the instalment of a Decca Radar, next came an electric kettle and then an electric toaster, which broke the camels back.

While I was on board there was a routine worked out and written down stating that if the radar was required the galley electrics had to be isolated to prevent an overload. If a position was required the radar needed to be shut down to get a reading from the Decca Navigator.

I passed for my First Mate's Certificate in October 1963. On passing my First Mate's exams I was appointed Navigating Officer of the Irish Oak in November 1963 (O.N.194596. GT 5049.02, NT. 2538.20, NHP 4400). I joined her in Cork and left her in Dublin 25th February 1964 on leave.

The Irish Oak was engaged on the usual North Atlantic run and on the usual grain and general cargoes. My wife joined me while we were discharging grain in West Hartlepool and remained on board for the trip around to Cork where we were to discharge part cargo. We had a very bad passage through the Pentland Firth where we were hove to for a tide.

Poor Captain Kirk was very concerned as my wife, Roisin, was pregnant and I was made attend to her during the bad weather while the old man did my watch on the bridge. The bad weather did not do her any harm. When my leave was about to expire Irish Shipping informed me that they were sending me to the SS Irish Plane, which was going out on a long term charter to the Far East. I declined as my wife was expecting our first child and I did not fancy leaving her for two years. So the company made me an offer which I could not refuse, either take it or leave it. So that was the end of my career in Irish Shipping Limited.

CHAPTER 13

James Fisher and Sons

I REJOINED THE British Shipping Federation and on their instructions I was sent up to Whitehaven to join the Shipping Company of James Fisher and Sons of Barrow-On-Furness who, at that time, along with their own fleet of coasters, were managing three ships for Marchon Chemicals Ltd. of Whitehaven. These ships were engaged on a regular run from Whitehaven lightship to Casablanca and back with rock phosphates for the factory in Whitehaven. The ships were named the Marchon Venturer (ON 187971, GT 1598.90, NT 748.61, NHP 321.4), the Marchon Trader (ON 187966, GT 1915.19, NT 903.47, NHP 304) and the Marchon Enterprise (ON 187970, GT 1598.90, NT 748.61. NHP 321.4).

The Venturer and Enterprise were under 1600 gross tonnage which was the cut-off figure for manning and harbour dues. The Trader, being over that figure, was obliged to carry a Radio Officer, 3rd Officer, 3rd Engineer and Chief Steward, while the other two were not.

I joined the Venturer as 2nd Mate on 5th May and was promoted 1st Mate on 25th August 1964 and served on all three of their vessels in that rank until 30th March 1965. I suddenly got fed up battling the Bay of Biscay, heading south in ballast while pounding and heaving in a most uncomfortable manner every trip and rolling heavily while loaded heading north again with two small heaps of heavy phosphate sand in the lower holds. For this reason, I requested a transfer to Sir John Fishers own vessels.

I found Whitehaven, on the Cumberland Coast very interesting as it was one of the oldest Ports in the British Isles with the most complicated system of pier harbours in the country. It was built originally in the early 17ᵗʰ century to ship out coal to Ireland and iron ore to ports in the UK. It was added to over the years and ended up being half a drying out harbour and half a dock where the vessels were locked in one half and dried out in the other.

They were still mining for coal in the 1960s, the seams of which extended out for miles under the Irish Sea. At low waters the locals would travel out over the sands with various types of vehicles and load up with coal which had broken off the underwater seams and washed ashore in the westerly winds. During the American War of Independence the American Admiral John Paul Jones laid off the port and bombarded the town.

On the 8th of April I was sent to Delfzyl in Holland to join their newly launched M.V. Eden Fisher (ON 307104, GT 1172.94, NT 684.19. NHP 74.5). She had all the mod cons, radar, Decca Navigator and was my first ship with VHF, Automatic Steering and hydraulic hatches. Only the officers were allowed to operate the hatches and as they were the first to be seen at the time on the Irish Sea they were a source of great interest and attracted a good deal of attention in all the ports we visited. Many bets were laid as to how long they would last, when the system would break down and cranes would be required to lift them off. But hydraulic hatches were there to stay and if and when there was an inevitable breakdown in the system the hydraulic connections were easily got at and pipes or hoses easily replaced.

The Eden Fisher was built as a general purpose coaster and had one hold forward of the bridge, and no 'tween decks. We went on charter to Atlantic Steam Navigation Co. Ltd., in Preston on their Preston to Larne service. At that time General Bustard was in charge of the company and I believe that Sir John Fisher had an interest in it also and that the firm had been born in Fishers office at a meeting in Barrow. It was believed, at the time, that General Bustard had made a deal with the War Office to operate three of their large landing craft and to keep them up to scratch and be readily available in good condition to the War Office at short notice. In fact they were acquired at the outbreak of the Suez Crisis and sent out there at very short notice.

Their names were the Empire Cedric., Empire Gaelic on the Preston run and the Empire Nordic on the east coast. They had large doors and a ramp forward where trucks were able to drive on and off, and with the bridge aft of a long main deck they were able to load trucks, cars, containers and flats on deck, using a Scotch Derrick built on the dockside for that purpose.

As far as I am aware Atlantic Steam was the first company in Europe to inaugurate a ro-ro and a container service on the Irish Sea and possibly on the North Sea. It was very much in its infancy in those days and trucks, containers and flats came in all shapes and sizes.

The Eden Fishers cargos consisted of this very mixed bag, as cargo was accepted as it arrived and was lowered into the hold first until it covered the ceiling. It was then lashed by the ships crew and the hatch closed and battened down. Then the remainder was loaded on top of the hatches where it was lashed in turn. There was no such thing as loading one container on top of another as very few were of the same dimension it would have been impossible to secure them.

In July 1966 I was promoted to Master and in total I served in nine of their vessels as Mate and Master. There were the three Admiralty war-built ships, the Race Fisher, River Fisher and Stream Fisher which were built as the Empire Jack, Empire Jill and the Empire Judy in 1943. During the war they were managed by James Fisher who eventually owned them. The Race and Stream were sister ships and the River was slightly bigger and still had her gun mountings in place on the wing of each bridge when she was sent for scrap. Their accommodation was not good. The wheelhouse was small with just room for about three people. They were fitted with an early type Sperry bouncing gyroscope fitted on a pedestal with a periscope protruding out of its top and leaning towards the helmsman and which took up the whole of the forward port side of the wheelhouse, and which hummed and groaned and looked like something from outer space or from Doctor Who.

The centre of the after end of the wheelhouse was taken over by two steering wheels and the electric steering motor with large gears and cogwheels which drove heavy chains that run over a gypsy on the shaft and down through the wheelhouse deck and then along the main deck where it was attached to the steering quadrant by an assortment of steel rods, shackles and heavy springs, to take up the shock resulting from the seas hitting the rudder. The small steering wheel which operated the steering gear was forward of the large wheel which operated the hand and emergency steering. This, when clutched in, was a direct drive to the gypsy. When using the larger wheel in bad weather one man stood on either side of it because of its kick and if a spoke managed to hook under any loose clothing and it caught you unawares it could throw you over the top of the wheel. As the wheel was as high as a man's shoulder it could do considerable damage unless your clothing carried away.

Steering gear in River, Race and Stream Fisher

You had to stand with your back to the smaller wheel as there was no room between that and the bigger wheel. This often caused confusion before new crew got used to it as they very often turned it the wrong way and when you started to turn it you had to stop the motion because if you didn't it would never stop until it was hard over. The noise out of the motor and gears when it was turning was bad and as the gears, slides and cogs had to be kept well greased you could only go into the wheelhouse dressed in working gear. There was also the danger of putting your hand on a moving part of the gears, particularly at night time and when the ship was rolling.

We were forever in trouble with pilots, especially when they boarded in the dark. No matter how many times we warned them they almost always managed to depart with some blobs of grease on their person.

This steering arrangement took over the whole after end of the wheelhouse. In addition, one corner was taken over by the flag locker and the other corner by a locker which held the Aldis signalling lamp, battery and other small gear. In front of the helmsman was the magnetic compass in its binnacle with its flinders bar and its port and starboard soft compensating balls on their brackets. In the forward starboard corner there was a small six-inch Decca radar. The only position for the officer of the watch was to wedge himself in between the radar and the binnacle. To move across the wheelhouse the officer had to either had to go outside and around, in front of the wheelhouse or ask the helmsman to move to one side. The windows were the old up and down type with the leather strap, similar to those in railway carriages which rattled like hell and in no way kept the draughts out.

The chartroom was directly under the wheelhouse and of the same dimensions, with a heavy wooden door on either side which opened out onto the boat deck. This meant that to get from the bridge and from the wheelhouse you had to use the outside ladders and step over a knee high wash bulkhead into the chartroom. The chart table took up most of the forward side and held the Decca navigator display consol. Along the aft end, there was a settee and on the deck there were the electric motors which supplied power to the radar, Decca, gyro and radio. Transformers were bolted to the aft bulkhead above the settee.

Having the chartroom below the wheelhouse was good exercise for the body and the brain, for at times, in close quarter situations you had to race down, scan the chart, lay off courses, and memorize courses, lights, buoys and channels. On one occasion, while coming west, down the English Channel in the Race Fisher, in a westerly gale off Start Point, the helmsman let her fall off course and we shipped a heavy sea which went right into what had been the lee door of the chartroom. When I went down to investigate in the darkness I stepped into the chartroom and into about a foot of water sloshing about it. I put my hand out and directly on to a transformer on the bulkhead. It belted me across the room, doing little damage to me but it did burn out all the motors and switchboard which in turn knocked out all the bridge electrics. So we had to rig oil navigation lamps and an oil lamp in the standard compass to proceed on the rest of our trip to Glasgow where all was repaired.

Work battered Stream Fisher

When I was Mate of the Stream Fisher (ON 169116, GT 745.60 NT 455.47), in 1965, we were sent to Workington to be fitted out to carry nuclear waste and I did not like what I was seeing. As we all had to do a special one-week course in Calder Hall, which was the research station attached to Windscsale, which is now Sellafield, we all had to be screened by security, and all were supposed to be British subjects. In an attempt to get myself out of this situation, of which the more I learned the less I liked, I told the head of security that I was Irish and that I was a member of the IRA. He told me that Irish were accepted in this case and that they had done a security check on me and that I was not an IRA man. The crew was divided in two and I was to do the second week of this course at Calder Hall, the captain doing the first week. They were collected at the ship each morning and we all got a commentary from them when they returned in the evening.

Meanwhile, work went on in the ship. Two pumps and two fans were secured in the after end of the hold with a maze of piping, two of which went up the mainmast. Then two large open-topped containers were secured in the centre of the hold, one on either side of the centre line and with a three-foot passage way between them. These were about the same size as a forty-foot container with no tops; they would come later. They were heavy as they were lined with lead. Then five, of what we called Lead Coffins, were lowered into slots in each container and a heavy lead-lined top or lid was lowered down on each container and secured to seal them.

A coolant was continually circulated through the containers and around the coffins when they contained the radio active rods, as they created heat and pressure. The coolant solved the heat problem but the pressure had to be checked regularly and released at least every twenty four hours and blown to atmosphere via the fans and up the mast. The ship had to turn off the wind to do this, similar to blowing tubes in a steamer, so that none of the contamination would fall on the ship. You could not do this if it was raining, as the contaminated rain water would then fall on deck.

I never did get to do the course at Calder Hall as I was transferred to the Leven Fisher whose mate got suddenly ill, and I never got back to the Stream Fisher until her second trip back to Workington.

The run was to Anzio in Italy, where she loaded waste from the nuclear power station at Medina, which is about twelve miles from the port of Anzio. I was told that on her first trip from Workington to Anzio she was carrying two scientists whose jobs were to observe and report. However, somewhere near Landsend the weather worsened and heavy movements were felt coming from the hold so the master decided to put into Port St. Mary, in the Isles of Scilly, to sort it out. It appears to have been sorted there but not before the two scientists jumped ship and informed the crew that they thought they were mad.

Concerning the course the crew went through at Calder Hall, as was later told to me, everyone was working in a clinical environment and a steady platform. They were given white overalls, hat, gloves etc., and were taught how to pass through decontamination rooms, take showers and go through an air trap which checked you for contamination and would not let you pass through until you were clear of all traces of radiation. You had to keep going back through the shower and checks until the door opened to freedom. You were always accompanied by an observer whose sole purpose there was to see that you touched nothing you were not supposed to.

They also demonstrated how contamination was spread by placing about ten familiar working tools, such as a hammer, a spanner etc., on a cleaned workbench in a cleaned room. Before the class was allowed in they sprayed two of the tools with a spray, such as that used by the police to spray money. They then invited one man in and asked them to lift up three tools as if to use them and place them back on the table and then to sit down. Next, they brought the rest of the crew in, one at a time, and asked them to pick up a couple of tools and to put them back on the table. When all hands had gone through this exercise they then switched off all the lights and turned on ultra violent lamps. Almost every person in the room glowed, as did the backs of chairs, the corner of the table, the door handles, noses, ears, clothing etc.

I do not know what the two scientists were expected to find on the Stream Fisher. Firstly, she was not a steady platform. Secondly, you could not get out of the hold to the one shower on board without touching something. Thirdly, there was no protective clothing and fourthly, there was no decontamination chamber.

The ship was a war-built seven hundred ton deadweight typical tramp coaster, built in a hurry with the bare essentials. She had a raised forecastle head, foremast abaft that, one hold the full length of the main deck covered by wooden hatch boards on sliding beams. To get up or down from the hold you had to climb an almost vertical ladder and through a square hatch with a steel watertight lid.

The master, mate, officers' saloon, galley, chief engineer, 2nd engineer and cook-steward all lived on the main deck and on the starboard side there were two toilets and one washroom with a shower. All doors opened out onto the main deck and in bad weather you had to ask the bridge to turn off and make a lee to get in or out of the toilets or washroom; the same had to be done to get the cook in or out of the galley on the port side. The ratings lived below deck and had slightly more room in their accommodation because the gunners' room, which had held four bunks, had been turned over to the crew after the war.

There was not much to do outward-bound as the coffins were empty of fuel, except to test and check the equipment. On arrival at Anzio, the dock area was cordoned off around the ship and a police watch maintained to keep the locals away. A crane lifted the two lids onto the quayside and the crew offloaded the coffins which were transported, two coffins at a time, to the nuclear power station at Latino, on World War II tank carrier, accompanied by a large police escort.

At Latino they loaded the waste rods into the coffins, resealed them and brought them back to the ship where they were loaded by the crew. Two more coffins were then loaded onto the road transport and sent off to Latino and this was continued until all the coffins had been loaded. When all was on board and as soon as the lids were on the containers and all was sealed tight it was my job, as mate, to start up the cooling system. They then lost no time in getting us out.

During the trip back to Barrow it was also my job to release the gases and blow them up the mast. This involved getting into my protective clothing which was my own boiler suit and working gloves and descending into the hold accompanied by my minder who was the captain. I then had to check that the pumps and fan were working and then my minder and I climbed the ladder to the top of the containers. There was a safety rail and catwalk on top to prevent us from falling off. I then opened a valve, ten in all, one for each coffin and released the pressure until the pressure valve showed zero. Then I shut off the valves and climbed down and stopped the fan motors, climbed up out of the hold, walked around and had a shower and change of clothing. My minder, who had marked all the points which I had contaminated on my rounds, then organized a work party to wash all the marked points. Well, that's what happened in theory anyway. What actually happened was as follows, as soon as we got out of the hold it was battened down, I took a shower, weather permitting, and sometimes the captain scanned me with the Geiger counter. That was on the good or reasonable days, on bad days you had to abort the whole operation.

There were plans to extend the operation to Japan, India and Canada but I went home on leave when we arrived in Barrow and I never went back to the Stream Fisher.

I have to point out here that, at this particular time, there were two types of agreement in the merchant navy to which you could sign on to. They were called A or B Articles. Most well established companies were on A Articles, which meant that you were on continuous pay from the time you signed a contract with the company until you left that company, usually after two months notice given from either party, and a flat monthly pay packet. B articles meant that you signed on to a particular ship and could leave after twenty-four hours notice in a UK port. When you signed off you were paid all your entitlements, holiday pay, overtime, Sundays at sea minus deductions and balance of wages chit plus a fully paid-up and stamped insurance card. This meant that you were free to do or go where you liked and were free from the company. On B articles officers received overtime payments and Sundays at sea on top of their wages.

A Articles were mostly used on foreign-going ships, while B Articles were generally used in the home trade. Home trade companies employed a cook on their vessels but did not supply the food. The crew gave the cook an agreed sum each week to do the weekly shopping. In the mid 1960s this amounted to two pounds and two shillings per man per week. How you lived depended on how good the cook performed. It was not unknown for cooks to abscond with this collection or to go on the beer during his shopping trip ashore and to arrive back on board with fewer stores than originally intended. It was known for ships' crews to go shorthanded without the cook after some very bad experiences. This meant that either one member of the crew was elected to do the cooking or that every man cooked his own grub. I never found either of these arrangements satisfactory and I always preferred to carry a cook.

I sailed with one man who was the relieving master in a coasting company which owned three colliers. When he was not employed as relief master, rather than take a mate's job, he always opted to revert to his permanent job as cook. He always maintained that next to the master, the cook's job was the best on board.

The Eden Fisher after delivery was engaged on the Preston/ Larne run on charter to ASN. The River Fisher was tramping on the coal and grain trade with the occasional short term charter to ASN or British Rail, with the Race on a similar trade. The Leven Fisher was on long term charter to Marchon Chemicals in Whitehaven with the three Marchon ships on the Casablanca/Whitehaven run. The Bay Fisher was engaged in the Felixstowe to Rotterdam ferry service which had been set up by Fishers and the Dutch Company "Packhuismistren" based in the Wallhaven. I was Master of seven of the Fisher vessels, which were the Bay, Race, River, Eden, Lune, Poole and Firth.

In July 1966 I was promoted master of the Bay Fisher which was then employed on the Holyhead/Belfast run on charter to British Rail. On 8th October, I was transferred to the Race Fisher in Felixstowe on the ferry service to Rotterdam. I then delivered her around the coast to Sharpness, where I handed her over to her new owners, Greenore Ferries, on 14th April 1967. She was then renamed "Owen Dubh" and worked out of the Port of Greenore in Carlingford Lough. I was immediately transferred that same day to the River Fisher, in Rotterdam, whose Master had become ill. She was tramping at the time on the usual coal and grain cargoes to various ports such as Southampton, Silloth, Glasgow and the Bristol Channel Ports.

M.V. Bay Fisher

In July 1967, I was transferred to the Eden Fisher on charter to British Rail on the Fishguard/Waterford service and then down to Southampton to the Lune Fisher again, on charter to British Rail on their service to the Harbours of St. Helier and St. Peterport, in the Channel Islands.

This was a very interesting run in the days before containerization and Ro-Ro. There was no such thing as cargo plans; almost all cargo was loaded as it arrived alongside. The mate had very little say in the loading and only a little say in the stowage. No one seemed to be unduly worried if cargo was left behind if it failed to fit in. We carried everything that could be consumed and used by an island population. Small stuff, such as vegetables, packaged foods, and drums were loaded and stowed on pallets. Bigger and more awkward machinery, motor cars and trucks were slung on board and placed in the hold or on deck. Then any available space around them was tightly packed by smaller goods. Needless to point out that there was considerable damage done to the cargoes in poor weather, as that sea crossing is well known for.

British Rail required us to carry one of their chief officers as pilot for the Southampton Waters. On one particular trip, from Southampton to Jersey, in a very large swell from the west south west, I was on the bridge nursing the ship and keeping the swell on the starboard bow to ease the rolling. This course would have left us on a dog's leg course out to the west of the Island, I was hoping to make a lee under Guernsey and then to run with the swell on the quarter to St. Helier, as was normal for us.

The pilot came up on the bridge at about 07:00 expecting us to be approaching St. Helier. When I explained to him what I was doing and what my intentions were, we chatted for a while and he informed me that breakfast was ready and that I should go down to get it. Thinking that I had explained everything to him, I left him in charge of the bridge while I went down to eat. I had not long sat down at the table when I felt the ship alter course and before I could get up from the table everything had slid off it and onto the deck, at the same time I felt the cargoes move.

When I got to the bridge and asked what was going on the pilot informed me that he had taken her around on a course for St. Helier as the course I had given him was too far west. I told him, in no uncertain terms, that I had explained to him what I was doing and that he had undone, in a few minutes, what I had nursed all night.

And that this was a ship and that she was not on railway tracks as all British Rail Officers seemed to imagine their ships were.

The reason I remember that incident so well is because when we opened the hatches there was a right mess below. That particular ship, the Lune Fisher, was one of the few Fisher ships fitted with 'tweendecks, and on the 'tweendeck hatches forward were stowed pallets of paint and other hardware stuff destined for some retail outlet. There was no cover on those hatches. Directly under the paint and in the lower hold there was a beautiful white Rolls Royce, stowed there purposely to protect it from the elements. What a mess; cartons and paint cans had opened and spilled their contents onto the 'tween deck hatch boards. The paint had then dripped through the hatch boards and down into the lower hold and all over the Rolls Royce. The car was discharged with the rest of the cargo and I never heard any more about the incident from anyone. I got the impression that no one in British Rail was worried and it was treated as an everyday occurrence. I did write a report and sent it to Fishers and I never heard any more about it from them either.

I received a message from the owners that I was to endeavour to put up with British Rail and their dockers' work practices, as they were very good charterers. One good thing about this slapdash way of loading and stowing cargo and the 'couldn't care less attitude' of the shore personnel, was that the ships' crew did pretty well out of it all. As we carried all sorts of foodstuffs in both directions and with this lack of care from anyone, we lived very well indeed.

I left the Lune Fisher at the end of October 1967 to sit for my Master's F.G. I started to attend the Nautical College in Belfast so that I could supplement my savings by drawing the social security. However, things did not work out. Political problems were beginning to get out of hand and by driving a car registered in the Republic I was leaving myself open to abuse. After three weeks in Belfast I transferred down to the Irish Nautical College in Dun Laoghaire, near Dublin. By changing from Belfast I lost my social welfare entitlement, as they would not pay it out in the south of Ireland. I was grateful for Fishers helping me out by paying me the loss as they did not have to, for I was always on B Articles and they were under no obligation to do so.

While attending College in Dun Laoghaire, I took a relief job as master of the SS Lock Linnhe during the Christmas holidays at the

College. The "Loch Linnhe" was a typical Collier, built before the war as a coal burner and later converted to burn oil in the boilers. She had a raised fo'c'sle, foremast on main deck, abaft the fo'c'sle and forward of No 1 hatch coamings. No 1 hold was in the well deck forward of the bridge housing and covered by wooden hatch boards on top of lift out beams which in turn was covered over with tarpaulins which were secured with steel battens and wooden wedges fixed to the sides of the coamings.

The bridge house was situated on the main deck forward of No 2 hatch. From the main deck you stepped through a midship door which placed you in a small lobby where directly ahead of you there was a door into the officers' saloon and on one side another door open to a washroom and toilet. Inside the saloon was a large polished table pushed into one corner and covered by a heavy cloth upon which there was large bundles of old newspapers and other reading material. Two large armchairs faced a big open coal fire situated off centre on the starboard bulkhead and a large oil lamp hung from the centre of the deck head. The fire had a tiled surround and was similar to an ordinary fireplace in any sitting room. It was set in a cement slab secured to the saloon deck to prevent it from moving while at sea.

On the portside, a door gave access to the skipper's bedroom and on the starboard side a similar door opened to the mate's bedroom. Directly over the saloon on the bridge deck was the wheelhouse and chartroom, and directly over the master's and mate's bedrooms were the port and starboard wings of the bridge. The wood decking of the bridge wings and the steel plating over which it was laid was leaking and dripping water down into the cabins and beds below in both the master's and mate's bedrooms, when it rained or sprayed heavily. The deck head in both bedrooms was peppered with small wooden plugs driven in over the years in an attempt to stem the drips, without success. This resulted in both men having to sleep in the arm chairs in the saloon.

Heating for this accommodation block came off the steam supply to the steering motor at sea, when the steering motor was on, and from the coal fire in port. Hot water for washing had to be carried from the stokehold.

In the wheelhouse there was a radar set, that had to be turned off if anyone wanted to boil a kettle; a voice pipe to the engine room for communications, a telegraph, a compass and binnacle and two steering wheels, one small one which operated the steering motor and a large wheel for leverage to turn the manually operated hand steering.

The steering, both steam and manual turned a shaft with a gypsy wheel on its end, which protruded through the aft bulkhead of the wheel house. The steam steering motor was situated outside the after bulkhead of the wheelhouse, on a bed which was supported by a heavy steel frame. Over the gypsy wheel was draped a chain which transmitted through rods, more chains and bottle screws, through sheaves and up and down and around corners to the quadrant on the main deck at the stern and which turned the rudder post which in turn turned the rudder.

During normal operations, the small steering wheel turned the shaft and gypsy and if, by any chance, steam was lost to the steering motor, you could, by a system of levers and sliding cog wheels in the wheelhouse, change over to manual steering using the big steering wheel. The noise of the steam steering motor and the chains over the gypsy and sheaves made sleeping hard at times.

Aft of the mid-ship house was the No 2 Hatch, similar to No 1 but much larger. Aft of that was the main mast and the house which contained, on deck, the engineers' accommodation, galley, messroom, toilets and washrooms. On top of this were the boat deck and various header tanks. Below the main deck there was crew accommodation and below that again was the stokehold and engine room.

Every trip, on arrival in either port and after making fast, the first job was to rig the water hose and start taking water. It was also the last thing to disconnect before letting go. It took me a few days before I took particular notice of this drill and when I mentioned it to the mate he replied that the chief engineer needed all the water he could get. So, when we got away from Belfast I asked the chief as to where all the water was going. He replied that there were plenty of leaks in the system and that it was losing a large quantity of water. I already knew of one leak on deck. That was on arriving or departing the berth when the windless was required for mooring. When the throttle was turned on I could not see the fo'c'sle head through the escaping steam. I figured that this bad leak could not be responsible for the loss of all that water, as steam to the windless was on only for a short while, but when the chief invited me below I was shocked. On the lower platform he handed me a small umbrella which was used to keep the scalding drips of water off your topsides. He had to use a fan to read some of the gauges. He then informed me that if delayed on a passage between the two ports for any reason, he had to change over to seawater to keep the ship going. He told me that this practice had been going on for some time and that the owners had been informed of the situation.

I also reported this to the owners and I informed them that I considered the ship unseaworthy. I requested to be relieved and handed in my notice. I was still on board the Loch Linnhe for another three weeks waiting for a relief, before I finally signed myself off in Belfast and forced them to relieve me. I was afraid that if the ship was lost for any reason, I would risk having my certificate cancelled, particularly if it ended up in an official inquiry. I was the only person on board who held any sort of certificate.

Within weeks of my leaving, I heard that the boilers had collapsed while she was leaving Belfast and shortly afterwards she was towed away for scrapping. The SS. Loch Linnhe may have been a fine ship in her day and well designed for the trade she was built for, which was for the carriage of coal. Apart from the fact that she was worn out, mostly from neglect, she was never built for the carriage of cargo on flats and a mixture of containers in those early days at the dawn of containerization.

I remember on one trip from Liverpool to Belfast we had six loaded flats stowed athwart ships on No 2 hatch. The flats were loaded with fifteen foot long, nine inch diameter heavy steel pipes with a tapered flange at one end, similar to sewage pipes. The flats were secured at each end, which overhung the hatch coamings, by hooks, chains and bottle screws to ringbolts on the coaming. The pipes on the flats were secured by light manila ropes, similar to heaving line stuff, which may have been enough to keep them on a lorry for transporting short distances. It certainly was not suitable for holding them in position on a rolling ship in gale when rounding the Chicken Rock. When one started to go others shot like torpedoes clean over the side until we lost them all and were left with empty secure flats on deck.

Another feature of the vessel was the loss of steam at times to the steering motor. When negotiating the buoyed and twisting outer channel at Liverpool in heavy weather she occasionally lost steering. This was caused by the seas shipped onto the main deck condensing the steam in the steam pipes running forward along the deck and bracketed to No 2 hatch coaming. As all the asbestos insulation had disappeared from all the piping the cold seawater turned steam to water and water would not turn the steering motor until it hammered its way through the motor and into the return line. This took time and it was hard on the nerves being left without steering, even for short periods, in a dangerous and busy channel. It was then that I decided to get out.

You may wonder how the owners got away with running substandard ships. In those days there was no such thing as Port State Controls and Harbour Masters had very little say as to what condition ships arrived in or departed their harbours. Surveys were carried out about every two years and they were very rudimentary. I remember on more than one ship the one lifeboat under radial davits was stuck with paint to the chocks and impossible to shift. Another company with four or five ships was known to collect articles such as life jackets, lifebuoys and emergency lights from around the fleet and place them on a ship which was due a survey. When the inspection was over they were transferred back to their own vessel. In other words, the inspector was surveying and passing the same equipment on all vessels. There were no such things as inflatable life rafts and the life jackets were of the old cork type, more likely to break your neck if you jumped into the water wearing it.

CHAPTER 14

Fishers of Barrow

DURING THE WAR, Sir John Fisher was in charge of coastal convoys and, with the contacts he made then, he obtained many government contracts after the war. A lot of his earlier ships were built with wooden hatch boards and shifting beams because he carried a lot of heavy and high loads that extended above the hatches' coamings from the lower hold. You could then put as many hatches and beams in place as possible and then build around and over the parts that protruded above the hatches and cover with tarpaulins. In fact one of their ships, the Sound Fisher, was built with hatch coamings which were circular midway along the deck to enable the ship to lift gun turrets whose barrels and turrets extended above the hatch and whose round turret fitted down the hatch.

When we were not carrying guns, rocket launchers, radar structures, prototype hover craft, generators, sections for submarines and aircraft, the ships were either on charter to British Rail, Atlantic Steam, Navigation, Guinness or the Ministry Of Defence, and in between times tramping with cargoes of coal, grain, stone, china clay, pit props or heavy lifts.

British Rail containers, at that time, were constructed like railway carriages with round tops which were impossible to stow on top of each other. They were constructed of wood in a steel frame with waterproofing material on the wooden roofs and came in 8-, 10-, 15- and 20-foot lengths. Using a Scotch Derrick for lifting on and off, it took four men on shore to hook them on and four more on board to release them. This was progress at the time.

Fishers also started up their own ferry service from Felixstowe to Wallhaven in Rotterdam. This was the beginning of the Ro-Ro, Lo-Lo and container service out of Felixstowe.

We loaded under the crane on the Sea Plane Pier which came off the beach at Landguard Point, at the entrance to Harwich Harbour. This was in 1966, before they started to develop Felixstowe and the shoreline up to Felixstowe Dock. During the development they shifted our berth into the small dock, which became very congested, and they then demolished the crane pier.

My favourite Fisher ship was the Firth Fisher. This was because of the Charters she used to get. She was built with the bridge amidships with No 1 hold forward and No 2 abaft the bridge was suitable for charter to Guinness in Dublin and the Ministry of Defence. She went on charter to Guinness every spring to relieve their three vessels for their annual dry-docking, and in early December for the Christmas rush, carrying barrels of stout to Pomona Dock at the top end of the Canal in Manchester.

In late summer, the Firth Fisher went to the Ministry of Defence for about two months to load ammunition in Barry Dock for dumping in the Beufords Deep between the Mull of Galloway and Northern Ireland. Naturally safety was a priority and we were only allowed to load a maximum amount of three hundred tons. I presume that this was to prevent us all from being blown into too many pieces. However, the money was good, as we had to discharge the cargo ourselves. For security reasons we carried three army or air force personnel, depending on which branch of the forces we were dumping for. We also took on two extra seamen to help with the extra work. There was never any pressure put on the ship and we could take as long as we wanted to dump. I used to work on dumping one hundred tons per working day, which was only a rough guide. It all depended on the type of cargo being discharged and the weather conditions at the time.

RAF one thousand pound bombs were the easiest to get rid of and required very little manhandling. We were supplied with special bomb slings which lifted four bombs at a time, one hook which fitted into a recessed lifting point in the bomb shell and lifted the bombs horizontally. They were then landed on a wooden platform constructed on the side deck between the hatch coaming and the bulwark, then unhooked and rolled over the side. The boxes of small calibre ammunition were hard labour, the wooden boxes were easier to handle then the steel. The American flash bombs were easy as were the mid section of rockets. The hardest to handle was the mixed bag we got from the police after they had one of their arms amnesties. We dumped everything from bombs, to Enfield rifles in their grease proof packing, to rockets, to machetes, to hand grenades, and from brand new to very old ordinance, such as cannonballs.

On board, when dumping, the crew placed the ammunition boxes into a specially built heavy wooden box, about six foot square and with sides of two feet high and a ring on each corner for lifting. When loaded, the box was lifted up by the ship's derricks and winches and landed on the platform, constructed on the side deck. Here, one side of the box was removed, two rings unhooked, one from each outside corner of the box, the two inboard corners were then lifted and the contents tipped over the side.

I was to stop dumping when the wind reached force five, so we spent a lot of time waiting around. I used to go to anchor off Bangor in Northern Ireland and lower the lifeboat where we went ashore to pass the time. At one particular time, the army personnel and I attended an open air meeting in the square in Bangor and at which the Rev. Ian Paisley gave one of his famous blasts to a large crowd of his followers.

Soon afterwards, I was instructed that I was not to anchor anywhere off the coast of Ireland as the terrorists were beginning to make inquiries about our cargo. From then onwards I anchored off the Scottish coast at Portpatrick or off the Isle of Man where we had some nice times.

Our motor lifeboat was the most frequently used boat in the coastal trade. In Peel, one summer evening, when some of the crew went ashore in the boat for the 'newspapers', they decided to have some refreshments in one of the local establishments. When they decided it was time to come back to the ship in the late evening they found that the tide had gone out and the boat was high and dry in the mud. Nothing new, it has happened to many seamen, numerous times in numerous ports and landings over many centuries. Every hotel ashore by this time had closed for the night, so the lads had to spend a long night hanging about waiting around for the boat to float again on the next tide at 06:00am. A very sorry looking bunch arrived back, tired and covered in mud which they picked up while trying, unsuccessfully, to push the boat down to the water. Although we, on board, had figured out what had probably happened, there was no way of getting in touch with the shore squad without making a big deal out of the situation, which we did not want to do. There was no such thing as mobile phones, no such thing as portable VHFs and very few fixed VHFs.

During these times at anchor, the crew had a nice little workshop going down in the hold. There were certain large shells which had their detonators removed and which, with a little persuasion, the brass shell casing could be prised off. There was a ready market in Barry for these brass casings. We had some scary moments, once in Barry, while loading, smoke was observed emanating from the centre of the already loaded cargo. The dock and the residential area around the ship was evacuated, the fire brigade and bomb squad called. After about four hours a smoke grenade was discovered to have been activated, in a box containing ten.

Another time, when loading bombs by shore crane into the ship, the sling broke and a bomb fell from about fifty feet. Its nose went through the ceiling boards and double bottom tank top but not through the ship's bottom. It did some damage, but not half as much damage as the dockers did to themselves, as they tried to climb over each other to get up the only ladder.

The third time was in heavy weather off the Smalls Lighthouse. One thousand pound bombs were loaded into specially constructed wooden bins in the hold. They were built of heavy timbers and shored off, and of a size which prevented the bombs from moving. As the weight of the bombs took up only a small area of the hold, the bins were built in the centre of the hold which left plenty of empty hold space ahead, astern and on each side of the bin. On coming up to the Smalls, the weather worsened and the ship took a dive which carried away the forward bulkhead of the bin. This caused all the bombs in number one hold to get adrift and one hundred 1000-pound bombs to roll loose around the hold. They threatened to go through the ship's side and something had to be done. There was no lights in the hold, the time was around midnight and we could not open the hatches because of the weather, so we had to rig portable light clusters on long leads down the trunk way and get down the ladder to try and shore off the bombs. We could not work from the level surface of the bottom of the hold, because the bombs were rolling around, so we had to cling from the ship's side like monkeys on the spar ceiling and jump down when we got the chance, recover a plank of timber and chock off the bombs as best we could. We then coiled mooring ropes in and around the bombs, where it worked its way between them. We finally got them, not secured, but comfortable, and the seas moderated as soon as we cleared the tidal race at the Smalls.

Firth Fisher

On another trip when bound from Rotterdam to Glasgow with a cargo of grain the cargo shifted while we were rounding Landsend. We hove to in a westerly gale and very heavy confused seas with a fifteen degree list to starboard until the wind abated and, with the assistance of the large bulk carrier Cape Howe and Her Majesty's submarine Tiptoe, we managed to turn round 180 degrees and head back towards Falmouth Harbour.

The Cape Howe manoeuvred close ahead of the Firth Fisher to create a lee while the HMS Tiptoe spread oil to windward to smooth the breaking seas. We managed, with the help of both vessels, to carry out the manoeuvre successfully and the Port St Mary lifeboat escorted us back towards Falmouth until she handed us over to the Falmouth lifeboat, which stood-by until we were safely in Falmouth Harbour where the list was corrected. From the commencement of this incident we had three different lifeboats in attendance, the Penlee boat first, then the Port St. Mary boat and finally the Falmouth boat.

HMS Tiptoe

At that time, grain cargoes were carried in coasters without shifting boards or feeders. There was always a free surface of grain in the holds as very few grain cargoes completely filled the hold up into the hatch coamings. Anyway in most coasters at that time the hatch openings were too large and the coamings too low to act as effective grain feeders. To contain the grain, one end of the bulk was sloped. The slope was then covered, from the lower end to the top, with loosely filled bags of the grain from the cargo and stepped up along the sloping surface of the cargo, supposedly to stop the grain from sliding. This bagging was always reluctantly done by a shore squad of casual workers employed for the purpose and was never completely successful. It was always the cause of arguments between the ship's officers and the foreman stevedore. In most cases the foreman went missing when the cargo was loaded and the ship was hauled off the loading berth by tugs standing by for such purpose and moored at the bagging berth. The pilot was then ordered by the stevedores before the bagging began.

As there was almost always a queue of vessels waiting to get in and loaded and as there was constant movement at the berth with up to six ships loading at any one time and maybe up to ten waiting to load, the idea was to get in and out and back to sea as quickly as you could so that you could get some sleep. Sleep could be hours away. The ship had to be battened down with hatch boards and tarpaulins and sometimes a long pilotage run had to be negotiated to the open sea.

If you tried to pull a fast one, by saying that you had engine trouble for instance, the tugs pulled the ship off to a stand-by berth. From there you had to inform the shippers when you were now ready to load. After the ship was inspected and passed you were then ordered to the back of the queue and start all over again. Meanwhile you had to explain to your owners the reason why you missed your turn and if the inspector wanted to, he could turn the ship down until the shippers were ready for you, thereby saving themselves the cost of having to pay out demurrage.

The Firth Fisher had a large cubic capacity and two holds, which meant that she was left with two large sloping bagged surface areas. One in the forward part of No 1 hold and the other in the forward part of No 2 hold. As we steamed down the English Channel we ran into a south-westerly gale at the Beachy Head and had it all the way to Landsend. I believe that with the heavy pitching into the head seas while coming down the Channel, the two bagged slopes of grain shifted. The forward facing slopes in No 1 and 2 holds slid forward and buried the bags in the bottom of the each hold. This movement of bags and grain then left an even larger free surface area of grain by lowering the top of the grain below the bottom of the hatch coamings, which had, until the shift, contained the grain.

As the vessel was heading into the seas, all the way down the channel she was pitching heavily at times and shipping plenty of water but as she was not rolling very much. The shift forward of the grain went unnoticed as the vessel remained upright. It did not show itself until we turned off a couple of points to round Landsend when at about 3am she rolled to starboard and stayed there, with a list of about fifteen degrees.

When we eventually managed to get back into Falmouth, after a struggle of about 48 hours, and opened the hatch covers there was very few burlap sacks to be seen in both holds. They were almost completely covered by loose grain. It took years afterwards for the authorities to make recommendations that coasters be fitted with shifting bulkheads when loading grain cargoes. I believe that the above incident on the Firth Fisher helped to change the thinking behind this decision.

One and a half years after the above incident, I again ran into trouble in the channel off Dover while still in the Firth Fisher. This was in June 1970, which happened to be a beautiful month, except for fog which covered the UK and the continent. The Firth Fisher loaded a heavy lift in Newcastle for the new power station being built in Fawley, inside Calshot Point in Southampton Waters. We had dense fog in Newcastle on the twenty-four hour run down to Fawley. On arrival we went straight alongside and the stator was lifted out and we were back at sea and into the fog again within four hours. The fog lasted all the way to Amsterdam where we loaded grain and we were out again into the fog, bound for Silloth.

At this time in 1970 there were no separation zones in force and no radar or VHF coverage in the channel. It was a free for all and only common sense seamanship was expected of everyone.

About one week before our arrival in the Dover Straits there was a collision about five miles south of Dover involving the tanker Texaco Caribbean and the cargo ship Brandenburg in which the Brandenburg was sunk. Shortly afterwards, another ship coming in to pick up her pilot at Dover drove up on the sunken Brandenburg and she herself settled on the bottom not far away from the Brandenburg. Since the sinkings a lot of salvage ships and their attendant craft had moved into the area and it was ringed with wreck marking buoys, diving boats, Coast Guard vessels and other attendant craft. Adding to the confusion was the usual heavy traffic negotiating the Dover Strait, and being thrown into confusion when they came across the scene of the disaster. In turn, in their confusion, they caused all other vessels in and around the area to make very hasty decisions, and all this in dense fog with very little control.

There were no regular broadcasts from Dover Coast Guard, and no compulsory VHF watch. Having negotiated the Channel twice some days beforehand, I was well aware of the situation that existed there, although I had only observed it on the radar while passing, and salvage craft and attendant ships, boats and wreck buoys were increasing in the area all the time. This accident had taken place in the middle of one of the busiest shipping lanes in the world and had to be removed as soon as possible.

So we steamed down, still in dense fog with a flat calm sea, on a course planned to take us midway between the salvage complex and Dover Breakwater. About fifteen minutes before we got to the danger area I needed to go to the toilet, so I handed over the bridge to the officer of the watch, leaving a helmsman and a lookout man on the fo'c'sle head on watch with him. I then went down to the toilet, which was on the deck below the bridge, on the port side. I must have dozed off because the next thing I heard, through the open port hole, was a prolonged blast on a ships whistle. I jumped off the toilet and was halfway up the ladder when a ship struck us on the port bow and knocked me off the ladder on to the deck. When I got onto the bridge and by the time I sorted myself out, the other vessel had disappeared into the fog. I never ever laid eyes on her. I instructed the second mate to broadcast a pan message and to try and get in touch with the other vessel to ascertain if she was alright. I instructed the chief officer to go forward and survey the damage.

The other ship was the Scandinavian registered gas tanker Unkas, who reported that she had suffered bow damage but was not in any danger and was proceeding on her voyage to Rotterdam. The mate reported back that the lookout was injured and that the ship was holed on the port bow, from about a foot above the waterline into the fore peak ballast tank and into the decks above it and stopped just short of the windless. In fact it was a perfect shape of a ships bow.

I decided to go into Dover to land the seaman and affect repairs. Repairs were carried out and the department granted the ship with temporary Certificate of Seaworthiness to proceed to the discharge port and then to the dockyard. We arrived in Silloth to discharge after an uneventful trip from Dover in calm seas with fog patches. It was a Saturday when we made fast under the silo and there was no work until Monday morning.

On Sunday, just about noon, in beautiful weather a chauffeur driven Rolls Royce drove onto the dock and stopped ahead of the ship where they had a good view of the damaged bow. After a period of time the driver opened the back, took out a picnic table and chairs, and set them up on a grassy patch under the ships bow. When all was ready, Sir John and Lady Fisher stepped out and with the chauffeur serving them and pouring the wine they proceeded to have a leisurely picnic.

It was then that I decided that two could play at this game. I arranged a barbecue on the beach, which was just astern of the ship and across the lock gates, leaving a few hands on board to receive Sir John.

I left the ship in dry-dock and went home on leave. While at home I received a letter from Fishers stating that as I had two nasty accidents within a short period of time their insurance underwriters insisted that I should revert back to chief officer for a while. I declined and decided that a bit of a change was required. I left the Firth Fisher and the company of Sir John Fisher and Sons Ltd., in Smiths Dockyard in South Shields on 26th June 1970, with no hard feelings.

CHAPTER 15

Coast Lines MV Wirrel Coast and Greenore Ferries

I JOINED COAST Lines MV Wirrel Coast as chief officer in August 1970, running between Liverpool and Newry, on a regular service, carrying the odd container, flats and general. As I had been running up the canal to Newry previously on the British and Irish steamship company's MV Dundalk, I was made pilot for the canal transit. We still picked up the local pilot at Omeath, opposite Warrenpoint, on the republican side, at the top of Carlingford Lough. The Omeath pilot took us up through the narrows to the Victoria Lock, which is the entry into the canal.

I stayed on the Wirral Coast for two months and then joined the company of Greenore Ferries which offered me a master's position and to whom I had already delivered the Race Fisher in Sharpness.

In 1971, soon after I left the Wirral Coast, the Newry Canal was closed to shipping and all trade was transferred down to Warrenpoint. I then joined Coast Lines MV Buffalo, which was on a regular service from Liverpool to Belfast.

Greenore Ferries operated four ships out of the port of Greenore, in the Republic of Ireland. They were the Owendubh, the Owenro, the Owenbawn and the Owenglass. They were situated on the south shore of Carlingford Lough, from where they operated a ferry service to Preston, Sharpness and Rotterdam.

The company had purchased Greenore Port from British Rail who had previously run a passenger, general cargo and cattle service from there to various ports in the near UK. British Rail had abandoned the port some years earlier because of the very strong tides across the entrance leading to the berth, and because of the big rise and fall of the tides, which at times prevented their vessels from maintaining a proper schedule.

Again, while I was in Greenore Ferries, containers had not yet been standardised and you fitted everything in as best you could and where you could best lash them. I joined the Owenglass in Preston and soon after went on charter to Coast Line on the Liverpool to Belfast run, and changed her name to "Irish Coast" as per the Charted Party. The Wirral Coast had since been withdrawn from service.

Greenore Port was an interesting port in that it is situated on a point of land on the south shore of the Lough, just inside the entrance and under Greenore lighthouse. The entrance to Carlingford Lough was notorious for its narrow twisted channel, sharp turns, strong tides and powerful tidal eddies which would set a ship in any direction and effect the steering.

The low water springs showed up what you were missing as you negotiated the channel and it was frightening, with jagged rocks on each side and with Haulbowline lighthouse in the centre of it all with its coloured sectors guiding you through. The sight at low water left you in little doubt as to what would happen if you made one wrong decision.

At high water, all the rocks were covered and naturally, everything looked different, but it did not change the dangers or widen the channel, as the rocks were still there just below the surface and, for the most part, unseen.

With the berth built at right angles to the main channel and its northern approach end jutting out into the main flow of the tides, it created a strong eddy across the entrance on the flood tide.

The best approach was to turn the ship beam on to the tide, just short of the berth, and to stop the engine to allow the tide to carry her up towards the entrance. The idea was to be in a good position so that, when she hit the eddy you were ready, with the wheel hard over to starboard, to give her full ahead on the engine as the eddy took her stern to starboard and pushed her head to port. Then you had to throw the helm hard to port when the bow entered between the quay and breakwater and out of the eddy while the stern was still in the effects of the eddy which was now pushing the stern to port and the bow to starboard and towards the breakwater.

If it worked, it got you in, out of the effects of the tide, and somewhere between the quay to port and the breakwater to starboard. It did not always work and there were plenty of scars on the ships and quay wall to prove it. During ebb tides, the approach to the berth was completely different as the eddy shifted to the other side of the berth and, although the tide was just as strong, you did not have the eddy to contend with. It was a great test of nerves and skill and a good training in ship handling.

I was master of their four ships and I can say that each one handled differently in different situations. Firstly, all were of different construction, with different lines and with different engines of different power. All were with hand-steering with a semi balanced rudder. Bow thrusters were unheard of and all had different methods of engine control and when you needed instant responses to your requests for engine demands, it did not always happen. One ship had the engine telegraph from bridge to engine room and a lot depended on the engineer on duty, as to how fast or slow you would get your order. The other three ships had bridge controls, and the most modern one had a variable pitch propeller and bridge control which I found the best to handle, as the main engine was turning all the time and it meant only to move the control handle on the bridge consol in one movement from ahead to astern and select your speed in the same movement. The other two were fitted with similar type bridge controls and were much different from the above system. Both had fixed propellers which meant that when you put the propeller into neutral you also caused the engine to stop because that was the way the engine was designed. To get the engine you had to give it a shot of air to release the shaft brake, wait three or four seconds, then give it another shot to get it turning and then adjust the speed and power to suit yourself. Sometimes in your anxiety or panic you missed the timing and the engine failed to fire. In that case, you could only start all over again, and meanwhile the vessel might still be forging ahead or astern or rapidly approaching a quay wall. You could only stand with the control lever in your hand and count in your mind the seconds, and slowly at that, before you could go through the next motion because, if you tried it too soon, you had to do it all over again, unless of course, the quay wall or the breakwater, which ran parallel and about fifty feet to the west of the wall, stopped her for you.

Then you had the chief engineer to contend with, when he started to shout about his air pressure and that the compressor was not able to put up with the demand imposed on it. This all happened while you were all alone on the bridge, trying to cope with all aspects of berthing and manoeuvring.

The company was running a service which had to fit in with tidal ports on the other side of the Irish Sea, so waiting for suitable and favourable tides and conditions was not an option for us. You berthed in Greenore when you arrived and that was it. While I was in the company I was negotiating with various UK foreign-going companies and in 1971 I departed Greenore Ferries.

CHAPTER 16

Texaco Overseas Tankships LTD

NEXT, I SETTLED for Texaco Overseas Tankships Ltd. I joined them in June 1971. At that time, in 1971, the Suez Canal was closed since the 1957 Six-Day War during which the Israeli army drove the Egyptian army back across the Senia Desert and west of the canal. The canal was closed for years afterwards and all traffic bound from the oil states in the Persian Gulf to Europe and the east coast of the USA had to go the long way around the Cape of Good Hope in South Africa. While the canal was open it had restricted the size of ships capable of negotiating it. At that time, with the canal closed, the size of tanker took off.

It made sense to tanker owners to increase the tonnage for the long haul around the tip of Africa, when the demand for oil was increasing, and it seemed that the canal was going to remain closed for a long time to come. Even if it did re-open the ships had grown so large that it would take a lot of reconstruction before it could take the bigger ships.

Ship owners were getting to like the larger vessels and began to talk about the 'Economy of Scale', which would make it more economical for them to go the long way around rather than to pay the canal dues. These very large crude carriers (VLCCs) could be manned by the same size crew as ships a fifth of their size and therefore would save money on manning.

I joined the SS Texaco Melbourne at Bahrain in the Persian Gulf in June 1971, as Junior First Officer, to train in Texaco procedures and to familiarize myself in tanker practices. The Texaco Melbourne was a T2 tanker, built in the USA in the early 1940s for the war effort. After the war, Caltex, before they changed their name to Texaco, purchased some of them to replace tonnage lost during the war. They then jumboized them. This meant that they had them cut in two, the two halves were then moved apart and a new sixty-foot section welded into the centre. They then lifted the centre castle containing the bridge and deck officers' accommodation and placed the lot on top of the boat deck on the poop. This increased their tonnage from 16000 to 22000 tons deadweight and also increased their speed and performance slightly.

When I joined her she was employed in the Far East trade, carrying refined produce. She was capable of lifting six different types of oil produce at any one time and was engaged mostly running from the Persian Gulf Ports and Singapore to Saigon with jet fuel for the forces engaged in the Vietnam War.

When operating on the Saigon run we were on a bonus due the fact that we were trading in a war zone. I mention this only because, a few years later when I joined a Japanese tanker the master, whom I relieved there, was also on the Singapore to Vietnam run during the same period, although we had not previously met. He was then serving on a Chinese-owned tanker which was registered in Hong Kong and he was on twice the war bonus we were getting from Texaco, but he was loading for ports in North Vietnam, the enemies! He told me that he loaded in Singapore, cleared for Hong Kong and cleared out of Hong Kong for ports in North Vietnam. Such is the ways of the world.

While trading in the war zone we were ordered to wait off shore until a convoy was formed and then we were escorted through the Mekong Delta and up the Mekong River to Saigon, accompanied by warships and fast armed launches while helicopters kept watch overhead.

The Delta was festooned with numerous low-lying Islands covered in dense growth where the Vietcong could take cover and launch attacks on the convoy. Some of the islands and parts of the river bank were laid bare by the American forces, with their liberal use of Agent Orange, the chemical which they sprayed from aircraft, affecting the foliage and the population alike. We, ourselves, were protected with flak jackets and steel helmets while the wheelhouse, and other strategic and exposed working areas on board, were protected by a wall of sandbags.

While negotiating up the sixty-mile river to Saigon we were always at risk of attack from the river banks. As we discharged our cargo ashore in Saigon we were under sporadic fire from the opposite bank and the well-armed military personnel on board dropped anti-personnel mines overboard at irregular intervals to deter Frogmen.

I was next sent out to join the S.S. North America at Ras Tanura in Saudi Arabia in the Persian Gulf as Junior First Officer to get experience in the workings of a Very Large Crude Carrier (VLCC). She was a tanker of 220,000 tons deadweight and I done two trips on her from the Gulf to Port of Spain in Trinidad, and then Back to the Gulf to load for Europe around the Cape of Good Hope. In Europe we called at Milford Haven, Europort, Zeebruge, Brunsbuttle and Southampton.

I joined her on the 24th November 1971 and paid off on 25th May 1972 at Southampton.

Each voyage around the Cape took approximately six weeks and another six weeks loading, discharging, time taken between ports and anchored off waiting for berths. In all, it took six months to deliver two cargoes. The first thing to hit me was the sheer size of almost everything, like the pipe lines, the pumps, the anchors, chains and winches. The accommodation and storerooms were spacious. All cargo was operated and controlled from a central control room. A big difference from my previous ship, the older T2 tanker, was where cargo handling was all manual and you had to stand over each tank and operate all valves by hand while loading or discharging and use all your senses like smell, feel, ears and sound.

The cargo control room on all VLCCs was inside the accommodation block, with a big electronic display of the cargo arrangement in which you could observe everything at a glance and had automatic control over all the valves, except the sea valves. It displayed all the pressure gauges, ullages and temperatures and you could smoke, drink coffee and even have your meals in the control room, if you fancied it, and it was air-conditioned. You had two cadets on standby with you, trouble-shooters, who could get on one of the bicycles kept handy with a portable radio and check things out on deck. In all, loading or discharging was far easier in the VLCC than in the T2. It was only when you had to repair anything that the T2 was easier, being smaller.

Promotion came fast during the Vietnam War, and in November 1972 I was promoted Chief Officer of the Texaco Saigon, a sister ship of the Texaco Melbourne, which was also engaged on the Saigon run from Singapore.

Then our trading pattern was altered on the Texaco Saigon and we were sent trading from Singapore to Darwin, Botany Bay and Cairns in Australia and Port Moresby, Madang and Lae in Papua New Guinea, Rabual in New Britain, and Kanas in New Ireland.

In Rabaul we were discharging cargo inside an active volcano, one side of which had collapsed leaving an entry into a weird but perfectly formed sheltered harbour. The only problems was that it was not very comfortable discharging highly inflammable cargo while hot ash was falling all over the place and flames flashing out of crevices high up the cliffs above us. It was a weird experience.

Ullages, or measurements, of the cargoes on the older tankers were taken with tape measure from the top lip of an ullage port built into the tank lid on each cargo tank, to the surface of the oil in the tank. Cargo temperatures were also taken from this position by lowering thermometers down to various levels. The tank lids could be swung to one side, or on some ships, lifted vertically to access to the tank.

During loading and discharging the tank lids were kept in a closed position and only the ullage port was used to observe the cargo and left in an open position to vent the cargo being loaded and to equalize the pressure when working cargoes. When not taking observations a spark arrester was placed over the six inch ullage opening. When you needed to check if the cargo in the tank was loading or discharging you placed a rag over the hole. If you observed the rag being sucked down the cargo was discharging, if it was being blown upwards the cargo was loading and if there was no movement on the rag the cargo was static.

On the newer VLCCs all cargo readings were taken in the cargo control room. In the early 1970s, there were no computers or electronic calculators. Before that time all calculations were done by longhand using logarithms or slide rule. Then a coffee grinder type of calculator came on the market. This was a manually operated machine which took a lot of twisting, turning and flicking from one column to another to get a final answer. It was so easy to make a mistake and there was no printout. This meant that you had to do the sums over again to check the answer. Still, it was easier than doing it longhand.

To calculate the cargo on board you got an API number from the cargo shippers in the loading port. This number indicated the amount of barrels in a long ton, at a certain temperature, and was issued by the American Petroleum Institute, hence the letters API. Next you took a ullage and a cargo temperature, then you corrected the ullage for the ship's trim, ship's list and temperature. This gave you the amount of barrels in each tank, which, when all tanks were added up and then divided by the API, gave the total amount of cargo on board in barrels and long tons. To check this figure you then had to look at the ship's draft (the depth of water the ship was drawing) from six positions: two forward, one on either side, two amidships, one on each side and two from aft, one on each side. These were then corrected for hog or sag and for the specific gravity of the water, taken with an instrument called a hydrometer, in which the vessel was floating. This would then give the displacement tonnage, which is the actual tonnage weight of the ship and everything on board and represents the hole which she makes in the water, in other words the weight of water she displaces. From this displacement tonnage you subtract the weight of the ship, fuel oil, lubricating oil, fresh water, stores, spares and crew. You now arrive at the deadweight tonnage, which is the actual weight of the cargo on board.

On a sea voyage, the cargo tonnage should never change but the amount of barrels on board is always on the change and is affected by the temperatures of the different climates and waters the ship passes through on the voyage. However, this does not alter the tonnage for, when corrected for temperature, the tonnage will remain the same.

A few days before arrival in the discharge port the steam would be put on to the heating coils in the bottom of the cargo tanks and the cargo maintained at a suitable temperature to allow the crude oil to be pumped ashore. If the temperature was too low it slowed up the pumping rate and prolonged the discharging time, if too high it created gases which could escape from the cargo and therefore causing it to lose value.

In the early 1970s, larger ships were fitted with Lodicaters which were usually supplied by the builders and designed specifically for that particular ship. These were designed to help the chief officer work out the stresses at strategic points of the ship's hull and were used by him before any transfer of cargo, ballast or fuel oil. This instrument was purely mechanical and allowed the mate to work out cargoes before loading, and to alter loading plans if the cargo or ballast on board at any one time threatened to overstress the vessel, by way of sheer or racking stress. It also worked out a finishing draft correct as to the information which was fed into it.

During any voyage, cargo or ballast and fuel oil was regularly transferred about the tankers to relieve stresses. They were fitted with fore and aft fuel oil storage tanks for this purpose. On arrival at a discharge port all the measurements, temperatures and specific gravity of the dock water in which the ship floated was taken and calculated once more in the presence of the receiver's inspector before any discharge of the cargo began.

Some years later we received more up-to-date calculators and computers which relieved the chief officer of much work. On the VLCCs, before discharging cargo, a maintenance plan was put in place for the ballast voyage back to the Gulf. All tanks had to be inspected on a rotary basis and there was nearly always repair work to be carried out to the cargo equipment inside and outside the tanks and pump room. During the discharge the tanks to be inspected were last to be emptied and, while they were being pumped ashore, the already discharged tanks were being filled with ballast water from the dock. This was to keep the ship balanced for, if you did not do that, you could over stress the ship and cause her to suffer damage to the structure or even to break in two, which has happened on too many occasions.

When the vessel cleared the last discharge port, tank washing commenced immediately. Firstly the empty tanks were washed clean, gas freed, inspected, scale removed and repairs carried out if required. Next, the cleaned tanks were filled with clean sea water while dirty water ballast, which had been loaded in the discharge port, before the tanks were washed, was pumped overboard. Except for the last few feet of oil contaminated ballast water in the bottom of the tanks, which would be transferred to the slop tanks and allowed to settle before the water under the remaining dregs of oil was slowly thieved from the slop tanks and discharged overboard, while the remaining oil and water left in the slop tanks would be loaded over at the next loading port. These dirty water ballast tanks would then, when emptied, be washed and gas freed and repaired.

It was our policy to leave the discharge port in light ballast condition and when the tank cleaning was completed we would take on heavy ballast for the long sea voyage around the Cape. Before arrival, at the loading port, some of the ballast would be discharged so that the minimum was left on board to be discharged while loading. Light ballast means the minimum of ballast water taken on board for the safety of the ship and depending on the weather conditions at the time. Heavy ballast meant extra water loaded to suit the weather conditions we might expect to be encountered on the voyage ahead.

Crude oil is very corrosive, as it is oil in its crudest state and carries a lot of sand and wax, which causes a lot of wear and tear, as it is driven under pressure and at high rates through pipes, pumps and valves. It also holds large amounts of sulphur and highly dangerous gases which makes it very volatile. It must be remembered that crude in its raw state holds all the gases contained in gasoline, benzene, jet fuel, diesel and every other oils which is extracted from it.

Before you can do any repair work, you must first wash the lines, pumps and spaces. Then, you must free them of all traces of gas. Wax congeals when mixed with sand in corners and gives off gases. This has to be dug out and removed by hand. When I first joined Texaco it was the practice to lift it out of the tanks in buckets and throw it over the side. This practice in no longer allowed and it is now held in sludge tanks and disposed of ashore. At that time you could have followed the blobs of wax and oil slicks all the way from Europe to the Persian Gulf and back and I mean all the way down the Bay of Biscay, the Atlantic Ocean, around the Cape of Good Hope, then up the Indian Ocean and through the Straits of Hormuz and the Persian Gulf. You could also follow the oil trails anywhere that there was a busy trade in oil, such as through the Straits of Malacca and across the Atlantic to North and Central America.

To prepare the tanks for entry or hot work, such as burning or welding, they had to be washed using high pressure jets, then they had to be gas freed by pushing air at high pressure down through the loading pipeline to the tank and through the Butterworth wash ports in the deck. Next, probes were sent down from deck level to test the gas and oxygen levels. If these were within a certain acceptable percentage level it was safe for the chief officer to enter. If not, the whole process had to be redone. This could take up to a day and even longer. When it was considered ready to enter the chief officer went down to the first level with a meter strapped to him, which took samples of the mixture and percentages of the oxygen. An alarm would sound if the instrument registered an explosive mixture. If it registered, you got out quick; if not, you proceeded cautiously to the next level. There were normally five levels to the bottom of the ship and the further you went down the more you became isolated from the deck and increased the unlikelihood of being rescued. You entered the tank through the tank lid on the deck and when you got to the bottom that entry point looked very small and distant. It always reminded me of standing in the middle of St. Paul's Cathedral and looking up at the ceiling and your only way out.

While there was someone down the tank there was always people standing by, on deck, with a breathing apparatus and keeping you under observation at all times. The chief officer was expected to enter the tank first, without breathing apparatus and to check every nook and corner for gas before a work party was sent down. It was always dangerous down there and nothing was taken for granted. I always considered the mate's first entry as the riskiest as to do a proper inspection you had to move away from the ladder and your only means of a quick escape. This meant that you had to climb up and over deep frames, some of them fifteen feet high, and through lighting holes with barely enough room to squeeze through. At times, the man on deck lost sight of you as you climbed and crawled from one section of the tank to another, with only a gas light torch for light and the standby man, with just a mirror reflecting the sun twenty meters down to where you were moving about.

All the repair work had to be done and ballast changed before you got to the loading port. A VLCC normally loaded about eighty thousand tons of water ballast while discharging cargo in port. This was called dirty ballast because it was pumped into unwashed cargo tanks. After completing any repair work necessary, the clean tanks were then filled with clean sea water and the dirty ballast pumped overboard. Dirty ballast was not allowed to be pumped overboard in port and there was very heavy fines imposed on ships, and even jail sentences handed out to ships personnel, for doing so.

Before arriving at a loading port you normally received a proposed loading tonnage. This was necessary because there were usually two or three different types of crude to be loaded or blended together and you could be loading cargo in one, two or three loading ports. All the time, you had to watch the stresses imposed on the ship. When cleared of the loading port, everyone settled down to a routine back to Europe. This meant normal sea watches again, and the deck crew was engaged in the deck maintenance, such as cleaning, painting, greasing etc. This work would have been neglected on the light passage outward bound while all hands had been busy ballasting, tank washing and repairing pipe lines, cargo valves, safety valves, measuring equipment, cargo pumps and numerous other jobs that always crop up and which cannot be carried out while loaded.

For the mate, it meant star sights in the morning and evening. These were the days before satellites and the GPS. There was a great deal of satisfaction to be got by working out the ship's position by using the heavenly bodies and the sextant. It also kept you more in touch with nature and the heavens. No doubt, the GPS is very convenient but it does little to activate the brain. Astronomical navigation kept you on your toes and making a landfall, after days or weeks without seeing any land, showed up your navigating skills for all to see. Computerized navigation, which has taken a lot of the risk out of navigation, as well as simplifying it, has also taken away the skill of dead reckoning and making allowances for the effects on the ship of tides, currents, set and drift. It has also taken a lot of feeling out of the job.

On the loaded passage the cargo could be sold many times on the stock market and when you departed the loading port you cleared with orders for the Cape of Good Hope, where you might then receive orders to proceed to the Caribbean or to Europe or Landsend for further orders.

At this time, in 1973, there were a lot of explosions causing severe damage on VLCCs in ballast passages and while washing cargo tanks. This was put down to static electricity caused by the fine spray in the wash water and electric charges of different polarity jumping across spaces to make contact with each other, similar to thunder and lighting in the skies. To cause an explosion there must be three ingredients available: gas, air and a spark. The gas and air must be mixed at the right percentages for a spark to cause them to ignite. If there is too much gas in the mix, it is too rich to explode. If there is too much air, it is said to be too lean. If it is the right mixture of air and gas, it is said to be an explosive mix.

To prevent an explosion, one of those three ingredients needs to be removed from the formula. It was decided that the gas could not be removed, as it was in the cargo. Static could not be removed as it could happen any time. This left the oxygen. As cargo or ballast was being pumped from a tank it had to be replaced by air or some other substitute for air. If that was not done the vacuum created inside the tank would cause it to collapse inwards. This was overcome by making the whole cargo area of the ship airtight and replacing the air with inert gases. Where was all that inert gas to come from, but from the exhaust gases from the ships funnel.

The SS. Texaco Frankfurt (ON 338001, GT 104615.85, NT 79057.21, and DT 200,000 SHP 28000 metric) was one of the first ships to be fitted out, in Lisbon, with this new Inert Gas System (IGS). A funnel valve was fitted into the funnel exhaust which shut off the exhaust discharge to atmosphere. Large fans drew it down through a scrubber unit, where water cascading down over baffles washed the impurities out of the flue exhausts and allowed the cleaned gases through to a pump room. This pushed the gas through a pipeline and a deck water seal, along a main deck line and branch lines on deck to each cargo tank. An automatic valve on a vertical mast on deck allowed the inert gas to escape to air, if the gases were not required in the cargo tanks. This mast was known as the *mast riser* and the valve was known as the *mast riser valve.*

During the voyage, this valve opened automatically, to allow the cargo gases to escape into atmosphere if the pressure in the cargo tanks increased, which would mainly be caused by climatic changes and/or an increase in sea water temperature.

It also worked in reverse and allowed air to return to the tanks if a dangerous vacuum was created for whatever reason. Although air was not recommended in the cargo tanks, there were times when it might be needed, such as a breakdown in the inert gas system.

These two way automatic valves were known as pressure/vacuum valves.

Pressure gauges were fitted in the control room and on the main IGS line on deck, to indicate and register the pressure in the line and the spaces on top of the oil cargo. If the pressure decreased, for reasons such as travelling through colder climates or colder seas, it was topped up with inert gas so that it always showed a positive pressure and therefore prevented air from entering the system. It was always preferable to have inert gases leaking out rather than to have air leaking in.

On vessels that were not fitted with the Inert Gas System, each tank was fitted with its own pressure/vacuum valve which allowed, through a network of pipes on deck, each tank to vent to atmosphere up a mast ventilator.

The deck water seal worked on the same principle as a toilet bowl, only very much larger. It contained a large amount of water to prevent smells or gases returning back through the line and was fitted with a low level and a high level alarm to warn if the seal was malfunctioning and not maintaining the proper water levels.

Apart from the deck lines and water seal, all the other parts of the system, scrubber unit, fans and fan motors were installed in a house especially constructed to house them, on the main deck beside the funnel. This house was about ten meters by ten meters by ten meters.

On completion of fitting with this Inert Gas System at Lisenhave Dockyard in Lisbon, the Texaco Frankfurt was ordered to the Persian Gulf to load for Trinidad. On the way to the Gulf, the system was tried out and worked satisfactory and all cargo tanks were inerted prior to loading, as was normal. While waiting to load, some boiler tubes in the main boiler were found to need maintenance and it was decided to do the maintenance work as soon as the vessel departed the loading port.

With the main boiler shut down for repairs the ship was able to proceed on the very much smaller auxiliary boiler. The auxiliary boiler was not able to create enough exhaust to supply the inert gas system. After shutting down the boiler, and allowing it to cool before entering, it was some days before engineers could inspect the tubes. They discovered that the tubes were in a worse state than expected and, while spare tubes were carried on board, there was not enough to replace all the damaged ones.

So, while the ship proceeded on the auxiliary boiler, which gave her a maximum speed of four knots, additional tubes were ordered to be supplied as soon as possible. The owners advised the ship to proceed towards South Africa to where they hoped to be able to get spares out.

I was at home on leave at this time and, three days before the ship was due to arrive, I was instructed to get over to Texaco headquarters in London where I was to be instructed in the use of the IGS, before joining the Frankfurt at Cape Town. Months before all this, the company had advised all senior officers of their intention to install the IGS in all their VLCCs, and in all future new buildings.

Roisin amongst the cargo pipelines

They had, months beforehand, supplied all their VLCCs with operational manuals and plans with instructions on how to operate the system. We all agreed to the IGS and took a keen interest in it for safety reasons.

Holding up the anchor chain

On my arrival in London, I was introduced to the Marine Superintendent who gave me a pep talk and told me that he was not the man that supervised the installation of the IGS but that he had read all about it. It turned out that he had read the same book that I had read. He informed me that the system was not working on board the Frankfurt at the moment, as the auxiliary boiler could not supply enough exhaust to feed the system, that everyone on board was familiar with the system and that the Chief Officer, who I was relieving at Cape Town would give me a rundown before he left the ship.

On the 12th May 1973 I joined the ship offshore at Cape Town with the new boiler tubes. When I arrived and was introduced to the chief officer that I was relieving, I told him that I would be glad if he would give me a run down on the IGS. He informed me that the system was not operational, that he had instructions to catch the boat ashore, and that he had left a lot of handover notes for me to study and all was self-explanatory. So, we shook hands and he headed off. The ship continued on her slow voyage to Trinidad while the engineers got on with replacing the boiler tubes.

I had told the captain that I had never operated the IGS before. He said that it was a great system but he knew very little about it, and that the chief engineer would instruct me. The chief said that it would take about five days to fit the tubes and get the ship back on full propulsion before we could operate the IGS.

Five days later, the big day arrived and the chief engineer and I waited in the cargo control room for the second engineer to complete his check list in the engine room. Finally, the phone rang and we were given the word to start operations. The chief then walked over and pressed the start button to begin the first stage of the operation and to start the fans in the IGS room.

At that moment, there was a massive explosion and when we ran out to investigate, we discovered that the IGS room was wrecked and there was a gaping hole in the main deck over the port fuel tank. Immediately, the crew had gone to emergency stations but there was no further reaction. We patched up as best we could and were ordered back to Europe for repairs and to call at Las Palmas in the Canary Islands to pick up inspectors prior to an investigation.

The IGS was supposed to end all such incidents such as this and there was a huge interest in shipping circles as to the cause and as to the reason why there was not a chain reaction through the whole system.

The enquiry revealed that the level alarms in the deck water seal had been neutralized in the engine control room and the water level in the water trap had fallen, which allowed the explosive cargo gases to force its way back through the seal and the deck isolation valve and into the fan room.

The cargo had been loaded in April, which is a relatively cool month in the Persian Gulf and, as the ship proceeded at slow speed southwards down the Arabian Sea, the Indian Ocean, past the Equator and the Mozambique Channel to South Africa, the air and sea temperatures increased which in turn heated up the cargo, which then gave out more gas.

On the mast riser there was an automatic pressure relief valve but this did not operate as the cargo-generated gas found an easier way out through the deck seal and past the deck isolation valve into the fan room. While the engineers were working in the engine room and the IGS was closed down, the deck seal alarms continued to activate and one of the engineers had stuck a match between the contacts to stop the noise of the alarm annoying them.

It turned out that they expected the mast riser P/V valve to automatically release excess pressure up the mast riser and they ignored the system until the word came from the engineers that the system was back on line again. They never thought to check the system or even to carry out the normal checks observed on all tankers not fitted with inert gas. In fact they were all lulled into a false sense of security. Even when the funnel flared off gases occasionally on the way down to Cape Town it never occurred to anyone to investigate. They scratched their heads and all agreed that they had never experienced that before.

When I went to London for the pep talk nobody told me anything I did not already know or read about concerning the IGS. I was told there that it was fool proof and all that I had to do was press a button and it looked after itself. When I arrived on board at Cape Town I was told more or less the same. I now believe that the crew was not familiar with the system, it was not working when they loaded cargo and everyone I met was of the same opinion that it was fool proof but never really fully understood how to handle it.

When the inspectors came on board to investigate, naturally I, as chief officer, was the first person they questioned. They were amazed to find that I never had any hands-on training with the system, nor did anyone else on board, for that matter. To cut a long story short we diverted to Europe and discharged the cargo in Rotterdam. The tank was cleaned on the way to and in Lisbon before dry docking there and finally coming out six weeks later with a whole new IGS. I was fully trained in the system while in Lisbon and after loading a few cargoes without mishap I was considered an *expert* and I was sent around the company's other VLCCs to lecture and demonstrate. I discovered that I was not cut out for that and requested that I be sent back as chief officer.

While waiting for a ship, Texaco asked me if I would be interested in doing a VLCC course in Holland. So, they promoted me to Master, just for the course, and I duly presented myself at the Netherlands Ship Model Basin at Wageningen for a three-day course on the ship handling and manoeuvring simulator of the N.S.M.B. from January 3 to January 5 1974.

I found the course very intensive, interesting and it compared very favourable with what I already had experienced and observed in the handling and manoeuvrability of VLCCs in light and loaded conditions and in different states of wind and tides. I must admit that I carried myself very well on the course and ran only one ship ashore and it was great to be able to go back to the drawing board and start the manoeuvre all over again and have another go at it.

In March of 1974, I joined the SS Texaco Great Britain where she was undergoing repairs in Verome's Dockyard in Rotterdam. The Great Britain started off with a bad reputation and never lost it during her lifetime with Texaco. On her maiden voyage to the Persian (Arabian) Gulf to load cargo and with some dockyard people still on board, they were testing the cargo pumps when one of the rotors burst out of the casing and ran amuck around the pump room wrecking havoc and killing three workers.

Shortly after that incident she was anchored off Bahrain in the Persian Gulf carrying out repairs. An Arab dhow arrived alongside with a squad of Arab workmen from the local repair yard. The ship was flying high at her lightest draft of approximately twenty feet, which would have given her a height of fifty five feet from the water to the main deck. When lifting the workers one by one from the dhow, fifty feet below, using the air powered pilot hoist, one of the workers fell off the hoist from near the deck level and landed on top of some of his co-workers in the dhow below. Three people were killed in this incident.

When I joined her, miserable January weather was being experienced in Holland, with snow and ice and bitter cold winds. The ship was shut down and we were all being accommodated in the Delta Hotel which was situated on the river bank, almost directly opposite the ship repair yard. We were ferried across at 0600hrs every morning and remained on board until 1800hrs, in a dirty cold ship, eating packed lunches supplied by the hotel. We were there for six weeks and it was one of the most miserable experiences I have ever had.

While I was there I first observed the smart looking Bell Line ships passing up and down the river with Bell containers and Waterford as the Port of Registry on their sterns. It was then I decided that I was not cut out to be a big ship man and I made up my mind that, some day, I would join that company.

But, to get back to the Texaco Great Britain, she was in to have large heavily built brackets repaired. These brackets were all under the main deck and connected the main deck beams to the ship's side frames and are a very important feature in the structure of any ship. About seventy of these brackets in various side tanks had fractured due to weakness or over stressing and needed to be re-welded. A special squad of welders had been sent to Norway from Holland to train for deep-welding which these brackets were going to require, as the steel in the structure was so heavy. When the welders had finished their job, the welds were then sonic tested and the test discovered that approximately thirty percent had either broken again or had not been repaired correctly, so the welders had to do the job all over again.

Meanwhile the dockyard bosses began by accusing me of having altered the stresses on the vessel by shifting ballast, transferring fresh water or fuel oil while repairs were being carried out and before all the brackets were completed, therefore causing the finished welds to fracture before all brackets could bear the weight together. I had copies of the ballast, fresh water and fuel oil layout on record and I insisted that we all go through the various tanks to prove to them that nothing had been touched, shifted or altered in any way. I also pointed out that it would not have been possible for me to have altered the weights and then put everything back as it had previously been, without being detected, when I had no power to run pumps. They were grasping at straws and were looking for a scapegoat.

We eventually departed the dockyard and proceeded to the Persian Gulf to load crude oil back to Europe. On the passage back to Rotterdam with a full cargo and in a position somewhere east of South Africa, a trace of oil was observed astern of the ship. After having checked everything on board and the hull, which we could see, we found nothing which made us arrive at the conclusion that the leak was under the waterline on the port side. As there was nothing we on board could do about it we maintained the course towards Europe spewing a trail of oil astern.

I went on leave soon after arriving in Europort and I never learned what happened or whatever became of the Texaco Great Britain after I had left her, nor did I care.

In all, I served in four VLCCs while with Texaco. These were the North America, Frankfurt, Great Britain and the Norway. These ships suddenly lost their mystery for me and I wanted to get out of tankers in general and VLCCs in particular, and I decided to look around elsewhere.

When I first joined the Texaco Bahrain I was just in time to witness the first bar to be installed in all Texaco vessels. Prior to this, beer was allowed to the officers and crew, which they took to their cabins to consume. This plan was advised by their spin doctors in an effort to combat the disease of "Tankeritas" and was taken on board by most British shipping tanker companies at the time. Tankeritas was a well-known phenomenon, a state of mind, particularly common in long-serving tanker personnel. It was caused by long periods without leave and the nature of the tanker trade, with only short periods in loading and discharging ports. These ports were very isolated, as they were normally situated well away from civilization, surrounded by acres of tank farms which made a run ashore for a quick break difficult, if not impossible.

To get through the tank farm you had to check in at the loading jetty end of the farm to be searched for matches, lighters and cigarettes and then wait to be conducted through the farm by security personnel. You went through the same procedure when coming back on board. The security always appeared to slow things down as if they did not want to encourage the crew going ashore. And it worked.

After one or two attempts at this you got the idea. Anyway, when you thought about it, it never was a good idea. There was never much outside tanker berths and most of the Middle East countries were dry anyway. There was also the problem that watches were never broken in tankers at loading or discharge ports. The effort taken to get ashore and back on board again invariably took a lot of time, and you still had to take up your watch when you got back and be back on board in time to relieve your mate.

At sea, tanker crews were inclined to retire to their cabins for long periods while off watch and to drink their allowance of beer, either on their own or in small groups. Engineers and deck officers did not mix that much in those days. I believe this originated in the old days in the changeover from sail to steam. The argument began by the deck gang telling the engineers (the black gang) that they got ships around the world without them for generations and the saying began that oil and water did not mix, i.e. deck and engine room personnel did not mix.

The installation of a bar, film shows and a swimming pool did help get over the problem somewhat, as drinks could only be had and consumed at the bar. These bars were very elaborate affairs, as becoming of a large petroleum company, and would have done justice to a passenger vessel. Even with these facilities on board it took a long time for the older hands to accept this more sociable approach.

When I became familiar with some of the investigators and specialists who arrived on board the Texaco Frankfurt at Las Palmas after the explosion on that ship they confided in me and told me that they had to attend special crash courses into the psychology of the handling of tanker personnel. Seemingly, they considered that I had not been long enough in tankers to become that much affected. However, I do remember one or two occasions in 1975, when I had served some four years in tankers, all the company ships were on economical speed of five or six knots on the long passages from the Persian Gulf around the Cape to Europe. One trip could take up to seven or eight weeks, where we all got into a deadly daily routine, and we resented anything which might interrupt this routine. I even got to hate the normal call off Capetown for fresh provisions, spares, mail, change of films or personnel, as it disrupted the routine.

On reduced speed with steam turbines the engine had to be run at full speed for about half an hour each day to blow out the boiler tubes and this became an occasion not to be missed with all hands off duty lined up at the ships rail to witness it. It was the high point of the day.

The ironic point is that some years after the introduction of the lounge bar on board ships the whole idea of drinking on board was reversed and drinking alcohol was barred on all vessels for safety reasons. I do not know what the conditions on board are nowadays but I imagine that it must have become very boring. While communications and leave periods have improved, crews have decreased, putting more workload on the remaining people. The turnaround time in ports have shortened so much now that crews never count on getting a run ashore and expect to remain on board from the time they join until the day they sign off. There is no such thing now as the old catch phrase "join the Navy and see the world" and work stress does not mean just physical work. All work and no play make Jack a very boring shipmate.

As chief officer on board, I was responsible for the training of the deck cadets and I had long discussions with them about my past experiences. I felt sorry for them as they very seldom got ashore for the period that they served on board. They were flown out, joined their ship, flown home again and the only part of the country they set foot on was the airport, which are mostly of the same design all over the world.

I told them stories of my experiences and particularly about the coastal trade, which they would not believe. I was not very popular with the recruiting department when I advised the cadets to go and join a company which managed a variety of ships. At that time, there were British companies managing and running a large variety of vessels such as Tankers, OBOs, Bulk Carriers, Freezers, Car Carriers, Timber Carriers, Gas Carriers, Cement Carriers, Passenger Vessels, Supply Vessels, long and short haul ships, and they endeavoured to give their cadets an opportunity to experience service on many different types. To my mind it was very unfair to confine a cadet, focusing his mind on just one type of carrier, as oil companies were prone to do, and also indoctrinate them into the particular working methods of that company. I could fully understand the reason why tanker companies were going through such a large turnover with cadets leaving the companies and the sea before their cadetship terms expired.

Another thing that I did not like about Texaco was the coded form that they required to be filled in and sent to head office from the vessel, after the completion of each loading and each discharge of cargo. On this form there was a long list of numbers with blank boxes beside each number. Each number was a question and the answer to that question had to be entered in the blank box beside that number. The answer in the box consisted of four digits. To find out what the question was you looked the number up in a special book and the answer from a long list of possible answers pertaining to that question in the same book and entered the answer in coded form in the blank box beside the numbered question. Each of the three senior officers, the master, chief engineer and the chief officer, had their own personal code book. Some of the questions and answers were common in all the books and there were also different questions relating to each officer's position and job. Typical questions on the form relating to me, as chief officer were: time alongside and fully moored, time hoses connected, time ready to load/discharge, time started to load/discharge, loading/discharge pressure maintained, reason for delay in mooring, reason for delay connecting hoses, reason for delay starting cargo, or reason for low pressures.

The questions went on like in this way, continuing to ask about cargo pump speeds and steam pressures received from engine room and as to whose fault it was that discharge or load rates were not maintained and what was the reason why the ship could not keep up the cargo pressures which the pumps were designed to do. There were so many questions that by the time you finished answering you had forgotten the answers which you had given at the beginning and was therefore liable to contradict yourself. I do not ever remember completing the report in one sitting, and it was too long and boring to check back through the coded questions and answers to bother checking your entries. This method of interrogation created bad feelings because each person's report overlapped and occasionally, unwittingly you involved one of your shipmates in something which he had no previous knowledge of. Of course, this was before computers on board ships and everything was done in longhand.

CHAPTER 17

Arklow Jobs

WHILE I WAS working for Texaco and home on leave, I was asked to take various relief jobs in and around the port of Arklow. One of them was as relief master of the local suction dredger, another as relief pilot for the port and then, some years later as relief harbour master. I enjoyed, up to a point, the time I worked as master of the dredger and as a pilot, but the position as harbour master was mainly routine and terribly boring and I disliked working for a committee, such as the Harbour Commissioners, which was comprised mostly of political appointees, local businesses and two port users, such as fishermen, who had very little input into the port operations.

Later on in my career I was still employed with Bell Line and working on a month on-month off basis, I shared the relief harbour master's job with Captain Jackie Byrne, who also worked for Bell Line and luckily Jackie was on duty with Bells while I was on leave and we were able to do the harbour master's job on our month off.

Jackie and I had grown up together; I was about three years older, but in the small close-knit community of the fishery and in the bosom of a large extended seafaring family, as children we all played together. Our mothers were sisters and Hagans from Rock View terrace. Although Jackie and I both decided to go to sea as a career we went off in different directions and came together again in 1977 when we joined Bell Line within days of each other, without knowing it. We were each master of different ships until 1993 when we began to meet up in Hong Kong as we relieved each other on the Euro Power and later on the OOCL Shanghai. After the liquidation of Bell Lines in 1995 we began to meet up again in the Gulf of Suez when we were relieving masters on the survey ship Blyth.

Relief pilot was a bit more exciting as the port was very prone to silting and tides were confusing. The Harbour Commissioners regularly attempted to take bigger ships into the harbour when at times it just was not feasible, due to silting at the bar across the entrance. The pilot had to constantly take soundings and watch the tides. While it took almost one hour to get out to and take in a vessel, provided the ship did not get stuck on the bar, it took hours to watch the tide gauge, as the tide was so unpredictable.

The tides at Arklow have a very small rise and fall, approximately one meter, and are therefore affected by outside influences, such as weather (from as far away as Fastnet, Sole and Lundy), local wind direction and heavy rains (which cause a fresh in the river) and barometric pressure. A high atmospheric pressure system reduces the rise of the high water predicted for that period and lowers the low tidal level. With low pressure systems the effect is the opposite, meaning that predicted high and low tides were higher. During certain predicted tidal ranges high water at Arklow would have double high tides, with the first tide being lower than the later and the second high might be up to one hour behind the first. These tides were also very much influenced by the above reasons and at times you could be waiting for the second high which might never materialize.

At this particular time, in the early 1970s, Arklow harbour was in a very poor state. It had hardly been touched from the time it had built in the early 1800s. The whole lower part of the town was built on sand. On the north side of the harbour there is a caravan park, built amongst sand dunes, that still exists today, and on the south side the Golf Links is carved out of sand dunes. The Avoca River cut channels through the sand dunes until training walls were put in place to contain the flow of the river and pier heads were built to protect the entrance. It was also expected that the flow of river water downstream restricted and funnelled by the training walls and the north and south piers would scour and deepen the river bottom. It did to a certain extent, but not quite as much as was expected, except in very severe rainfalls which only occurred approximately once every twenty five years or so.

The last time it hit was in 1986 when the tail-end of Hurricane Charlie swept across the Atlantic and dropped all its water locally. It carried away bridges, sunk and washed boats out to sea, flooded vast tracks of land, scoured the river bottom to the extent of removing wrecks long covered by silt, caused sections of the river walls to collapse and almost undermining the pier heads. The training walls were built with very little foundations and constructed with dry stones without cement and capped with granite slabs. This prevented the engineers from dredging for they feared that the walls would fall into the river. To facilitate ships, jetties on piles were built out from the quay walls into deeper water. This flow of fresh down the river from the high hills and mountains not very far inland keep an almost constant flow downstream, except in droughts and big tides, when the flooding tide pushed the water back into the river. The early planners did not understand that fresh and salt water do not readily mix. The discolouration of the water seen at sea off the entrance is just the thin edge of a wedge between fresh and salt water, and fresh water flows over the top of salt water and mixes in its own good time.

While skipper of the local dredger, the Treadagh, when not dredging we were engaged at one time working at an outflow pipe which carried waste from a factory to sea. The pipe had broken off and the dredger was engaged in digging a trench along the pipe to expose the break and repair it. To do this we had a large air compressor on deck with divers working an air lift on the sea bottom over the pipe. With this method the divers were able to lift the sand and stones almost to the surface where the tide carried them away to one side. While this was going on I was learning to dive in the hopper of the dredger. I soon advanced to the stage where I was able to dive down and observe the divers working on the bottom. Later, when they were shorthanded, I would give them a hand under their supervision.

We carried an air compressor on board to top up the divers' air bottles, but one day the compressor broke down and rather than miss a days work the head diver decided that he would get the bottles recharged at the factory, which was duly done and then returned them to the dredger. He also came back on his own as something had come up and the second diver was unable to accompany him for that day. Out on the site I was asked to go down with the lone diver who was trying to make up for lost time. We had found and uncovered the break in the pipe and rigged a tripod with a chain block at each end of the pipe section. The broken section had been moved to one side and the new section ready to put in place and the flanges bolted together, a matter of an hour's work. As there were only two of us diving we agreed to work one at each end of the pipe. As the visibility below was very poor we would be working out of sight of each other. While I was working at the flange under the tripod I became unconscious and could not remember what happened next. My mate at the other end of the pipe had finished his job and came along to see how I was doing. He discovered that I was no longer there and assumed that I had gone up. On his way up he discovered me tangled in the top of the tripod with my face mask and mouth piece not in place. He got me clear of the tripod and, as he had a dry suit, he inflated it and we shot to the surface twenty feet above. The fresh air must have revived me for I came to as soon as we reached the surface.

In trying to find out the cause we figured that my mate was using an air bottle which had been filled the previous day on board while mine was one of the bottles filled at the factory. When we went out to the factory we discovered that the bottles had been recharged in a contaminated atmosphere and where there was a strong smell of ammonia which was used in large quantities at the factory. We reckoned that I must have inhaled a lot of ammonia which under pressure which had the effect of knocking me out. Whatever the cause, it was a close shave.

During one of my periods on leave, the Milford Haven trawler, the Jade Star Glory, came ashore on reefs just off the beach north of Cahore Point, which is about twelve miles south of Arklow. The crew abandoned the vessel in two life rafts in a gale force SE wind. The Arklow lifeboat was launched and in a hard punch south in heavy seas she picked up the two life rafts with the help of flares deployed from the boat.

On arrival back off the bar at the entrance to Arklow the coxswain was advised to proceed north to Wicklow and land the rescued in that port, as the breaking seas across the bar made it too risky for the boat to enter. The coxswain, local fisherman, Michael O'Brien, opted to take the risk because it was decided that one of the rescued men was in such poor shape that he might not survive the longer journey up to Wicklow. I was down on the pier head with others that morning at 0300 hrs as the lifeboat made her approach.

While we waited and watched there was a bit of a lull in the seas and the coxswain took the opportunity to go for the entrance. As she was about four lengths from the smoother water and passed the point of turning back, we, on the pier, heard a roar of a breaking sea behind the high sea wall of the pier light-tower that we could not see but knew full well what it was. Then it came into our line of vision and over the top of the wall and what we saw scared us for the men in the boat. A wall of white breaking water hit her beam on. She was then lost to us as the wave buried her and she disappeared under it as it pushed her sideways, across the entrance. We all thought she was gone but suddenly we saw her reappear, shake herself, race the last few lengths and she was in. All the rescued were landed safely and all recovered from their ordeal. For this rescue the coxswain was awarded the RNLI Medal of Gallantry.

My connection with the Jade Star Glory began when I was next home on leave from Texaco. Four months later, I was asked by a scrap merchant who had bought the wreck if I would find a crew for his tug Sir Milne and take her down to the wreck to offload the fuel oil that still remained on board in, as yet, the undamaged fuel oil tanks. This was 1973 when there was a worldwide shortage of oil, when the Suez Canal was still closed, tankers were having to negotiate the long passage around the Cape of Good Hope, when OPEC were beginning to flex their muscles and motorists everywhere had to queue up to get a gallon of petrol. The economy was coming to a standstill and fuel oil was been rationed out to industries, ships and the fishing industry.

The Jade Star Glory had just left her home port of Milford with full tanks of diesel oil, still intact after all that time on the reef with a pinnacle of rock stuck up through her fish hold on which she moved on spring tides. Our first priority was to get the oil off to prevent pollution, lighten the wreck and refuel the tug. The owner had men working on the wreck off and on, depending on the weather, preparing salvage pumps and hoses in preparation for offloading the oil. The tug was a beautiful little craft which was one of two he had bought for scrap and cannibalized one to make the other seaworthy. I have no information as to the origin of the tugs but I was told that both tugs were built for the invasion and to especially to assist on the beaches at Normandy. They would certainly have been very suitable for that job as they were built with double bottoms and fore and aft ballast tank. In other words they were double-skinned, which enabled them to discharge ballast if they found themselves grounded on the beach. I remember that the scrap merchant's engineer was able to stand on the control platform and stick his head out over the fidley and observe everything going on. She had an oil burning boiler and the chief was also doing the job of fireman. She was certainly the handiest little steamer I have seen.

The first time I was contacted to take her down to the wreck we were not very successful. We went down to the wreck site, got across the reef and alongside. We were delayed connecting up the hose and getting the pump started, meanwhile the weather was worsening, the swell increasing and the high water gone. So we aborted the operation, took the salvage crew off the wreck and headed home.

The weather did not improve and we missed another chance during that spring tide, I went back to sea for a period of five months. While I was away there were two more attempts to recover the oil and pull the trawler off. They managed to recover some of the fuel oil but had to abort both attempts. On one occasion they had to request a helicopter to lift some of the salvage crew off the wreck as the tug had to depart in a hurry. In another attempt, endeavouring to navigate the reef the tug came down heavy on the rocks and damaged her propeller and the propeller guard. They managed to get her off and she limped back to Arklow on the damaged propeller, with the help of a square sail made out of a tarpaulin rigged on the mast. In port, divers discovered that there was just one and one half blades left of the four bladed propeller and even they were in poor shape. The owner had her then taken to Dublin, docked and then fitted with the propeller and guard from her already cannibalized sister.

When I arrived back home on leave again after five months the Sir Milne was lying in the dock waiting for the right conditions to have another attempt at the Jade Star Glory's salvage. Things had changed at this stage of the operation. It had all dragged out for too long, time had not improved the wreck; it was getting to the stage where it was time to cut the losses. This was to be the last attempt. In addition, the tug had enough fuel on board only to get down to the wreck. It was imperative that the scrap merchant, now the owner, got the fuel out of the ship, as he was liable for any pollution it might cause.

So I recruited a crew one night in the local pub and told them that departure time was 2300hrs, so as to be down at the wreck in good time before the high water springs. I told them that we had to get the oil off her to lighten her and enable the tug to pull her off. I did not tell them that we had to get some oil off her as the tug would not have enough remaining on board for the return back to Arklow, the nearest port, and if we failed to do that the tug was liable to end up on the rocks alongside wreck.

So we left port on time, had a snack and I told the motley crew to relax down in the fo'c'sle and that the engineer and I would take her down. We had an uneventful trip south, it was a lovely June night with a low swell, and I called all hands when we were making the approach to the reef. I was trying to time a swell to ride over the reef. When I saw a swell approaching which I thought might do the job for us I ordered full ahead on the engine and when we were surfing over the top of the reef I stopped the propeller to allow her way to carry the tug clear to the inside.

Tug "Sir Milne" entering Arklow towing the
salvaged trawler "Jade Star Glory"

The last Steamboat into Arklow Dock

But I must have underestimated in the darkness and she came down, not too heavily, under the stern. I thought that she had not done much damage so I decided that now that I was on the inside of the reef the sensible thing to do was to make sure we got some fuel on board so the we had some chance of getting back to Arklow, regardless of what else might happen. There was still two hours before high water and everything was ready on board the wreck to pump the oil.

Meanwhile I had a minor mutiny on my hands. Coming out of the lighted fo'c'sle and into the darkness the crew were temporary blinded and did not know where they were. There was a lot of shouting and confusion and demanding to know what was I up to. When I told them what I was doing they demanded that I should get to hell out of there if we could. It did not go down too well with them when I informed them that we could not go anywhere until we got some fuel.

The oil transfer went without hitch and no oil leaks were observed from either the wreck or the tug. While transferring oil we were also busy rigging towing lines and preparing the trawlers own warps for stand-by tow lines. As it was breaking daylight we were ready to start our first attempt, which was not a success. We did manage to turn her head ninety degrees but she was still held by the rock pinnacle up through the fish hold and a smooth rock inside her port quarter which prevented her from turning further.

Then, I do not know exactly who, suggested that we rig the trawlers warps from the foremast head and that the tug would pull from off the starboard beam and rock the trawler off the pinnacle which was now the only thing holding her. The rock under the port quarter would help hold her from turning and increase the leverage caused by the pull of the tug from the top of the mast. We tried a steady pull in the planned direction and while the trawler listed over somewhat it was not enough to clear the pinnacle holding her, but the idea was good.

We had a man carefully observing the tide ashore on a small pier and, when we received word from him that the tide seemed to have reached its peak and was now steady before starting to fall again, we decided that we were left with little time to play around. I backed the tug towards the trawler until the tow line was slack in the water and drove the tug ahead at full speed and cleared the deck in case the tow line parted. It sang when the line became taut, rocked the trawler, but she still held firm. From those on board we learned that it almost did the job and one more, harder pull from the same direction might succeed. So I backed the tug almost to the trawler to allow us to get a longer run at it with the slack of the tow line coiled on the after deck. The tug forged ahead on full revs and again the towline sang and I could see the mast of the trawler bending towards us and I said to myself, that's it, we've blown it. But it worked, the pull that bent the mast had exerted enough leverage to pull the trawler over the rock slightly before the mast started to crumble, she was free. Now it was only a matter of tidying up and making ready for the tow back to Arklow. When we arrived back at the harbour the harbour master allocated us a safe berth inside the dock, for which we were grateful.

When the harbour master arrived at his office the next morning and saw the trawler was sunk at her berth, he was not too pleased, and demanded that she be raised and removed immediately. The pumps had stopped for some reason during the night and allowed the water to increase. However she settled on the bottom of the dock with the water level below the main deck at low waters, which meant that there was no great problem raising her again. She was eventually towed away for scrapping.

Getting the trawler off the reef was not an earth-shattering achievement as salvage operations go. We were operating on a shoe string with an underpowered tug, casual crews with no previous salvage experience, and I probably broke every rule in the book. You could never get away now with what I got away with then. While there were rules and regulations on the books, as I was well aware of, there was little enforcement unless there was an accident, which thankfully there was not. I enjoyed every minute of it, even when the crew threatened mutiny when they wanted to go back home and I had to tell them that there was not enough fuel remaining on board.

CHAPTER **18**

Motor Tanker Sea Royal

AFTER HAVING LEFT Texaco, and while still at home looking around for a job, I was offered a position by the master of a Japanese-owned tanker to become chief officer on his ship, with the intention of relieving him as master. I agreed, and joined the MT Sea Royal in Milford Haven in January 1975 and was promoted master in March of that year. The Sea Royal was a tanker of 75,000 tons DW, and when I joined her she was one year old. Her ON was 367902, GT 43827 and BHP 20300. She was a lovely modern vessel and was easily the best tanker I was ever on, well laid out and fitted with all mod cons of the time. A simplified IGS, an excellent pump room and pipe line arrangement and a speed of 16 knots.

Tanker Sea Royal

The owners were the Japanese Sanko Line, she was registered in Singapore and the official head office was in Monrovia in the West African State of Liberia. We were told on board to give the Monrovian address to anyone making complaints or enquiries, or for any official business.

Before signing on the vessel I was required to sign a contract for six months. It included fixed compensations in dollars for the loss of any limbs, eyes, fingers or ears etc. This contract was then sent to Monrovia for *processing!* Luckily, we were completely accident free to personnel while I was there.

The senior officers both deck and engine were European and not all of them could speak English, the crew was all Filipino. In and around the mid 1970s there was a hiccup in the oil business, tankers were laid up all over the place, VLCCs were all on slow speeds to and from loading and discharging ports. Often, on arrival at these ports they could expect to spend weeks at anchor waiting to get alongside to load. There was a worldwide go-slow in the oil business.

However, the Sea Royal had been fixed on a long term charter with the American oil company Aramco before the slump and was contracted to maintain a speed of 16 knots. If the ship fell below this speed the company was liable to fines and penalties.

Handling a young grounded Albatross

Aramco, with a lot of their own ships laid up and few cargoes available, were trying to force Sanko out of the contract with penalty clauses. They did not manage to do this while I was there, and while we were racing around the world on full speed, passing other tankers steaming at low economical speeds, we were often signalled, asking us where we were going in such a mad rush.

I was promoted master while loading a cargo of light Arabian crude in the Persian Gulf which we delivered around the Cape of Good Hope to Wilhelmshaven in Germany. We loaded two cargoes in Ras Shakuir in the Red Sea for European ports and on one occasion, loaded there for Genoa in Italy. Not very far apart, as the crow flies, but with the Suez Canal still closed it was over a month's voyage around the Cape of Good Hope. On each occasion, while entering the Red Sea through the Gulf of Aden we called at Djibouti for bunkers and dry stores.

I had arranged to be relieved in Genoa. However, after six months accident-free we got into a bit of trouble while berthing there. The discharge berth was very tight for a ship of our size. I was surprised to see large white villas, with washing hanging out in the sun, all built close to the boundary wall around the tank farm and overlooking it, built on a steep hillside, each with a lovely view overlooking the busy harbour.

While we were manoeuvring alongside with the assistance of two tugs I ordered the engine room to prepare the IGS and cargo pumps for discharging cargo, as was normal practice. Suddenly there was a blast of black sooty water-contaminated exhaust out of the funnel which rained down on everything and everyone. With a fair breeze blowing on shore you could observe the lovely white villas and the washing getting blacker and blacker. It was the same with us on the bridge and on the tug boats and the white uniformed officials waiting on the quayside. It took about thirty minutes before the deluge was stopped as we could not stop the main engine because we needed it to manoeuvre. By that time all about the ship was in a very poor state with watery exhaust soot running down walls ashore and bulkheads and faces on board.

Naturally, there were all kinds of complaints and threatened claims for damages made against the vessel and I felt very sorry for the German master on the quayside, waiting to relieve me. What a way to join or leave a ship. As my flight was booked for early the next morning, I handed everything over to him that afternoon, ship's papers, official books, crew papers, cash and the safe keys and combination. The only advice I could give him was to send off all the complaints and claims to the post box in Monrovia where it would all be looked after.

I left the ship that same evening while they were discharging the cargo and there was a big cleanup in operation on board and on shore. I stayed in a hotel close to the airport as I was flying out very early the next morning. I always felt that I had got out of town just ahead of the posse. I never heard any more about the incident.

One of my biggest problems was getting enough U.S. dollars to pay the Filipino crew, whose contract demanded that their balance of wages be paid to them at the end of each month, even at sea. U.S. dollars were not always easy to get, some countries would not part with dollars and when you did manage to find some you tried to get as much as possible to cover for a few months, as you never knew where you might go next or when you would be next able to top up. I never felt easy about having so much ready cash on board and about the crew hoarding their wages until they got a chance to get ashore, which was never easy on a tanker, to send the money home. In one way, you could not blame the crews as numerous other crews had been caught out with dodgy companies going bankrupt and crews losing months of hard-earned wages. But I always thought that there must have been a better way of doing things. In and around the Gulf of Aden there was a high risk of pirates and on one occasion we were chased by a gunboat which was unable to overtake us before we closed the land and they gave up the pursuit.

When I left the Sea Royal in Genoa in early July 1975 I had no intention of ever going back to Sanko as I had had enough of the dodgy contracts we were required to sign. In addition, it was a very lonely life on board, for the previous two months I was the only person that spoke English, I could not hold a conversation with anyone and all orders were given in broken English. However, as there was still a shipping slump on I was compelled to phone Tokyo for a job. They told me that there was no jobs at the moment as a lot of their ships were laid up. Shortly after that, Sanko Line was declared bankrupt and was wound up, to be eventually resurrected under new management some years afterwards.

CHAPTER 19

Taursues 3 Denholm Ship Management

DENHOLM SHIP MANAGEMENT Ltd of Glasgow was advertising for men as they were expanding their management business, in spite of the slump. I signed a contract with them on 30th October 1975 as chief officer. When they asked me to join a tanker I said that I would but that I hoped that this would be my last tanker, as I was getting a bit tired of them. They replied that that would be fine.

So a whole British contingent of officers and I were flown out to the island of Guam in the Pacific Ocean, where we were joined by a Filipino crew to take over the Monrovian-registered Liberian tanker Taursues 3 (GT38912, BHP20700, ON4473, DT 65,000). The ship had been built for and owned by the Danish Mearsk Line and had been sold on to the Greeks about ten years later with a loan from The Chase Manhattan Bank. Unfortunately for the Greeks, they had been caught up in the tanker slump and had failed to maintain their payments to the bank. The bank then seized the ship in Guam and contracted Denholm Ship Management to run the vessel for them.

When we arrived the ship had been in port for some time and the crew had taken over the vessel and refused to allow any person on or off. They had large placards hanging over the side and bridge stating that they would not allow anyone to touch the vessel or cargo until they were paid their wages. It turned out that they had not been paid for months. There were a lot of negotiations going on and security around the vessel. We refused to board until the crew were paid and had completely left the ship. We did not want to interfere and we sympathised with the Greek crew.

After a week in a hotel, which overlooked the ship, we saw the crew go ashore and when we were satisfied that the Greeks were happy with the result of the dispute, we went down and took over. The first thing to greet us, as we stepped onto the deck, was the barking of dogs which were locked into a deck store. They turned out to be the crews' pets, two German Sheppards, who did not take kindly to this new crew. We quickly slammed the door shut and agreed to sort the dogs out later after we sorted ourselves out.

The ship was loaded with 60,000 tons of a blend of Arabian heavy crude and naphtha which had to be heated to enable it to be pumped. Before doing anything I had to familiarize myself with the cargo layout, pipe line layout and pump room layout. When I looked at the ships plans they were naturally all printed in Danish and had all been overwritten in Greek longhand. That was not all. When we finally worked a discharge plan and put it into operation, we discovered that the Greeks had done a fair bit of sabotage to pumps, gauges and valves etc. We kept finding these problems as we progressed through the discharging routine which delayed us considerably. I was under pressure to get the cargo out as there were other ships waiting to come alongside and I had completely forgotten the two dogs. When I enquired of the Filipino bosun as to what had happened to the dogs he said that we had all had them for dinner.

Immediately after clearing the harbour we stopped with engine trouble and drifted about for some hours while the engineers repaired the fault. We could not anchor as the depth of water under us was about one thousand meters and no ship carries enough anchor chain to reach that depth. Guam is a volcanic island and rises almost vertically from the ocean floor.

We were bound for Bahrain in the Persian Gulf on a course which was to take us across the Pacific Ocean to the Philippines through the Bohol Sea, across the Zulu Sea to the Balabac Straits, then down the South China Sea past Singapore and through the Straits of Malacca, then across the Bay of Bengal around the tip of Ceylon, now Sri Lanka, up the Arabian Sea through the Gulf of Oman

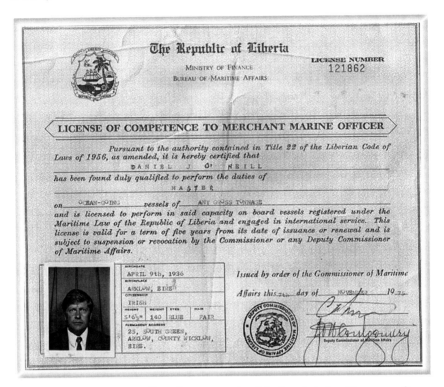

Liberian Master's Certificate required before joining Taursues 3

and the Straits of Hormuz and into the Persian Gulf. But this was not to be. In the middle of the Zulu Sea we came to a grinding halt. The engine stopped and there were no spares on board to repair it. We drifted for five days while we waited for a tug to come from Singapore, again we could not anchor as the water was too deep. This was not the best place in the world to be broken down with engine trouble, as it was a well-known pirate nest and stopped as we were, we were sitting ducks. We took as many precautions as we could to repel boarders and practised with high pressure hoses and fire monitors, which were left, rigged and ready for use. However, we never saw another craft of any sort until, after a wait of five days, the Dutch tug Zuiderzee appeared over the horizon and took us in her charge. Seven days later, after fine weather and an uneventful tow, which gave us plenty of time to wash and clean out the tanks, sort out and test all the cargo pipes and pumps, we arrived in Singapore only for the ship to be arrested by the bailiffs. It appeared that the last time that the Taursues 3 was in Singapore, with the previous Greek crew, she had departed rather suddenly without paying harbour dues, ship Chandlers and other services. It took a week to sort out the problem while we lay at anchor in the harbour and then we were on our way to Bahrain.

On arrival at Bahrain we were arrested again and a writ put on the mast. This was caused by the same problem, unpaid bills. Two weeks later, we were alongside, loading crude for Darwin and Botany Bay in Australia and then back to the Persian Gulf to load for Guam again, where I was signed off to go home on leave after five months and six days. I flew home to Dublin via San Francisco, New York and London in April 1976.

I was put up for one night in a hotel in San Francisco to await a connection the next morning for London. I went by taxi from the airport to the hotel which I paid in dollars, no problem there. When I booked in at the hotel desk and offered cash to the reception I was told that only credit cards were accepted. I never had a credit card in those days and I was not aware of any seaman in those days that carried one. I knew that they were in common use in the USA at the time, but in Europe, the UK and Ireland they were still thin on the ground. This was all happening at 3am and I had to wait about two hours while the manager was called and arrived as he was the only person authorized to accept cash.

I had to get up again at 7am to make the connection to London and when I arrived at the desk in the airport I was informed that I had to pay an airport tax to get on board the plane. I explained that I had flown in from Guam the previous day and that I did not know anything about tax as my ticket had been paid straight through from Guam to Dublin. I was told that Guam was considered to be inside the USA and therefore the flight from Guam to San Francisco was an internal flight which did not require an airport tax, but as I was departing the country from San Francisco I would have to pay the tax there. Fine, but now I am back to square one again, I have on my person only cash and the desk cannot accept cash, they would have to get the manager. I almost lost my flight waiting for him and, when he arrived, he cleaned me out of every cent I had on me and I boarded the plane in San Francisco with not a penny in my pockets. I had left Guam with what I thought was ample cash but I had not counted on having to stay overnight or having to pay for taxis or taxes in San Francisco. So I had to wait until I arrived in Dublin before I could cash a cheque and purchase refreshments.

My next ship with Denholms was the M.V. Avon Bridge. They kept their word; she was not a pure Tanker. She was an OBO. OBOs were dreamed up by ship-owners to cover all eventualities and could change from lifting bulk cargoes to liquid cargoes, depending on what was available at the time, and also to minimize the amount of time the ship travelled in ballast. The reason they were called OBOs was because they were capable of loading oil, bulk or ore. Certain adjustments were made by the crew, who called them *orrible bloody objects.*

There was a number of these type of large vessels built in the 1970s and none of them had a good name among seamen, but owners liked them. They had nine cargo holds, which could with a certain amount of adjustments, alterations and much work on behalf of the crew, be converted into oil tanks by making them air and gas tight, re-opening and sealing various pipeline connections, fitting and reconnecting heating coils, sensors and automatic gauges, and re-opening pipeline suctions and hatboxes. There were two cargo oil slop tanks, used to contain dirty oil and water washings from the main cargo tanks, one on each side of the main pump room. The cargo holds/tanks were self trimming and built diamond-shaped with the corners cut off. The top of the diamond was cut off to take the coamings which supported the hatch covers and strengthened the opening, which allow large grabs access to the holds for the discharge of bulk cargoes. The lower part of the diamond was cut off to allow the grabs a level surface to remove the bulk cargoes from the bottom of the holds, with the minimum of trimming. The widest part was halfway up the hold and tapering towards the bottom and top. This was to reduce the free surface effect in each tank when loaded with liquids and to make them self-trimming when loaded with bulk. All the bulk cargo would slide to the bottom where it could then be easily removed by grabs if ore, or by grain elevators if the cargo was bulk grain. The insides of all the tanks/holds were flush and were free from stringers, floors, brackets and frames. All those strengthening structures and frames were outside the tank/holds, and inside the water ballast tanks, double bottoms and void spaces. This arrangement meant that there were large void spaces between each tank and in effect the ships were double-skinned.

Ballast was carried in side tanks, on each side of the holds. These side water ballast tanks dropped into the double bottom ballast through drop valves and were pumped out through the double bottoms. Ballast water was also carried in the fore and aft peak tanks. Bunker fuel oil was carried in the forward fuel deep tanks, which were abaft of the fore peak water ballast tank, and aft in deep tanks on each side of the engine room and in double bottoms under the engine room.

Vertical ladders gave access from a trunkway between the coamings of each hatch to the bottom of each hold/tank and beside these another similar ladder allowed access to the bottom of the void spaces between each hatch/tank. The coamings of each hatch were three meters above deck level and served as feeders while loaded with grain and reduced the free surface effect when carrying oil cargoes. Iron ore never reached deck level because of its heavy weight. The hatches themselves were of the ordinary Macgregor-type hydraulic in two sections and moved horizontally sideways on tracks port and starboard over the side decks to open up the holds.

A tunnel, which was square in shape and was built into the keelson which ran fore and aft in the centre of the ship between the port and starboard double bottoms and under the cargo holds/tanks and void spaces from just aft of the forward collision bulkhead to the pump room. The main access to the tunnel was in the aft end at the bottom of the pump room. There was also access through a watertight hatch in the forward void space which was also used to ventilate it. Each void space between the holds was constructed with escape hatches from the tunnel. A pair of tracks ran the full length of the tunnel which carried two bogies on which you could ride, keeping low, but which were intended to carry tools, spares and sections of pipelines and was propelled by hand and fitted with brakes to hold them in position. All the pipe lines ran through the tunnel and it also gave access to the cargo, ballast, stripping line valves and to the heating coil valves and lines.

Discharging an oil cargo from an OBO was far easier than a tanker as all the suctions were sunk into the double bottoms in a hatbox and with the ship in stern trim all liquid cargoes drained aft into the hatbox from where it could be pumped ashore without having to use the stripping pump and lines. The tunnel was also a very scary place as there was always oil and water sloshing around the bottom and it always had to be well ventilated and tested for gases. But it was comparatively easier and cleaner to work at pipes and valves than on tankers. It was also very claustrophobic working under 150,000 tons of cargo. On the other hand, discharging, an OBO was easier to work than that of a pure tanker.

But it had one problem, while loading or discharging, which was not there in a tanker. That was the free surface effect which the oil cargo had if it was loaded or discharged in such a way that there were more than three slack tanks at any one time. On numerous occasions OBOs have flopped over to one side while working cargo alongside, if they fell off the jetty they risked breaking the hoses and causing an oil spill and if they fell onto the jetty they caused damage to the jetty or vessel. This was because of the way the OBO was built compared to the tanker. The OBO was constructed with nine cargo holds/tanks which could hold about 16,500 tons of crude oil in each, while the lower part of each tank tapered from about ten feet or so from the bottom and reduced the free surface area and the upper part of the tank tapered from about ten feet below the deck and then up into the ten foot high hatch coaming which also reduced the free surface area. The space between extended out to almost the ships side and this left a comparatively large free surface area and where, if the ship took even a small list, a large volume of liquid would flow to that side. The maximum amount of tanks that could be worked at any one time was three and all the other tanks had to be either full to the top or emptied, otherwise the ship would flop to one side or the other.

The OBOs were built with nine hold/tanks in a line one behind the other from forward to aft under the main deck. The widest section of the hold/tanks extended almost from one side of the ship to the other. On the VLCCs there was seven rows of tanks, each row was

The ill-fated OBO Denbighshire (ex Liverpool Bridge)
which was lost with all hands in the South China Sea.

Silver Bridge steaming south in moderate weather in Mozambique
Channel, Indian Ocean with full cargo of 150,000 tons of Crude Oil.

divided into three separate tanks, so that there would be n°1 centre, n°1 port and n°1 Starboard, and so on down the deck, from forward back to the pump room. This means that there were twenty-one tanks in a tanker against nine in an OBO. In the OBOs, each tank held around seventeen thousand tons each, so that when the oil level was more than ten feet above the bottom of the tanks the combined free surface would cover a much larger area than the many smaller tanks and subdivisions incorporated into purpose-built tankers.

Changing from oil to bulk or from bulk to oil was a major job. At one particular time I discharged a full cargo of 150,000 tons of Iranian Heavy Crude in Rotterdam's Europort. At that time, in 1976, the authorities were clamping down on tank washing and cleaning and had banned it along the regular trade routes from Europe to the Gulf and others. However, there were specially designated areas where they allowed it. One of these areas was to the north of Iceland. Why this particular area, I do not know but we were ordered there from Rotterdam to tank clean and then load a full cargo of coal in Amsterdam. We were allowed two weeks to get back to the loading port.

On the way up to Iceland and as soon as we departed Rotterdam we tank-washed and then we gas-freed, next we had to go down the tanks and remove the residue, this was a mixture of solidified sand and wax which would not flow and blocked the suctions. As the ship went north the sea temperatures dropped and made everything more difficult. It all had to be lifted out by hand in buckets and dumped over the side. When the tanks were gas free and clean, the suctions were blanked off, hatboxes covered with perforated steel plates covered with burlap so that water would be allowed to drain into the box while cargo would be prevented from doing so.

Next the heating coils would be disconnected from their inlet and outlet flanges and holding down brackets. These heating coils were in two parts, one on both sides of the centre line, and big enough to heat 16,000 tons of crude oil. They were then lifted up and secured under the hatch covers. The hatches were then opened sideways over the side deck where the final touches could be put into securing the coils. Then you were ready to load bulk. The reverse procedure was carried out when changing back to oil, including one other very important job. Bulldozers were lowered into the bottom of the hold when the discharge grab was working the last few hundred tons to feed the cargo to the grab. Both the grab and the bulldozer often caused damage and it was very important that any damages were noted and repaired.

But nothing is always as simple as it sounds. A lot depended on how long the ship had been on oil cargoes. If it had been for any great length of time the dogs on the hatches would have seized, the hydraulic jacks, chains and chain guide wheels might also be seized and heat would have to be applied to get it all moving. When rigged for oil everything had to be sealed and made gas tight and remained untouched, unless a leak was detected.

Each ship was supplied with an instrument called a Lodicator. This was a box which, when opened, contained a drawing of the vessel and was divided up into every compartment, hold and tank. Each compartment on the plan had two knobs which allowed you to feed in the amount of tonnage which you calculated was in each space. The Lodicator was an early type of computer which was designed for one purpose, to calculate the stresses while loading or discharging, ballasting or transferring cargo on board while the ship was at sea or in port. It could not be transferred to another ship as it was programmed only for that vessel and was fed with information supplied by the shipbuilders.

In the old days, you had to calculate all this by hand but as the ships got bigger and loading or discharging became faster and quick turnarounds in port were the order of the day, it became too much so the Lodicator was developed. It was a godsend for the chief officer and for others. But one thing worried me about it. The instrument was supplied with information when the ship was new and I never saw one being readjusted to take into account any alterations made to the ship, such as repairs, or for the wear and tear and old age.

For instance, iron ore cargoes were very hard on hull stresses while oil cargoes would be comparatively easier. Some OBOs could spend up to 85% of their working life on oil while others could spend far less. This meant that two sister ships of the same age could be very different structurally, with one suffering from severe metal fatigue while the other might be reasonable. I can never remember the Lodicator being adjusted to take any of these reasons into account. There were very heavy shear stresses imposed on these types of vessels, particularly when loading iron ore when only alternative holds were loaded and the other holds remained empty. The rate of loading ore also had a big stress factor and this was impossible to calculate.

Too many of these type of vessels disappeared or were lost at sea through mysterious circumstances. One ship that I had been on in 1977 broke in two and sunk at her berth, while loading iron ore in Sepiteba Bay in Brazil in the 1990s. By that time, I was well out of her.

The final resting place of the OBO "Kowloon Bridge"
on the Stag Rocks off the Cork Coast

In July 1976 I was sent out to Newport News on the east coast of the USA to join the M.V. Avon Bridge (O.N.341253, G.R.T.79316.57, N.R.T. 67330.64, B.H.P.29000 port of registry, London). She was to load a full cargo of 150,000 tons of grain for Japan. When I went on board, just before noon to relieve the chief officer, he was just starting to load the cargo in n° 3, 5 and 7 holds and beginning to discharge ballast water from the permanent ballast tanks to counteract the cargo being loaded and so as to relieve the stresses imposed on the ship's hull. He had already made out a loading plan and a deballasting plan to suit the loading pattern and speed of loading, as was normal. He handed over to me and in the late afternoon he went ashore to catch his plane home as everything was proceeding normally with cargo being loaded and clean water ballast being pumped into the harbour.

Sometime after midnight I looked over the side to check the discharge flow of the water from one of the permanent water ballast tanks and discovered that the whole dock in the vicinity of the ship was covered in black crude oil. Immediately, all operations were stopped and the coast guard was informed. They threw a barrier around the dock to contain the oil and then prepared for cleanup operations. Meanwhile the vessel was arrested while an investigation was carried out. The master and I were also under house arrest and informed that we would not be released until the owners had deposited one million dollars to cover the cost of the clean-up.

During the investigation it was discovered that a bulkhead plate between the n° 6 cargo Tank and the permanent ballast tank had fractured and allowed crude oil, which had been the previous cargo to be loaded in the ship, to leak into the then empty ballast tank. It had gone undetected at the time and ballast had been pumped into the tank as the oil cargo in the adjacent tank was being discharged. By the time the vessel arrived in Newport News the oil in the ballast tank had settled on the top of the water ballast and remained undetected until the ballast water got low in the tank and the oil reached the suctions.

What a mess! I was sort of getting used to being arrested since I had joined this company. Anyway, the rest of the contaminated water ballast was contained on board where the contents were pumped into the slop tank, the water thieved off and the oil held on board to be loaded over with crude and pumped ashore with the next oil cargo. On the way to the discharge port in Japan the contaminated tank was washed out and gas freed and ready for repairs. We left the oil coated berth to be cleaned up by the United States coast guard.

We were next sent down to Port Hedland in west Australia to load iron ore back to Japan where on completion of discharge there we were ordered to change back to oil while proceeding to the Persian Gulf. On arrival there we loaded crude for Taranto in the foot of Italy, which meant another trip around the Cape of Good Hope. After discharging in Taranto we were ordered to tank clean and then proceed to Naples for dry-dock, where we eventually handed over the vessel to new owners.

After a period of leave I was next sent to Venice to join a sister ship which was discharging oil there. This was the Silver Bridge (O.N.358746, G.R.T.79378.71, NRT58721.17, DT (cargo) 150,000 Tonnes). On departure from Venice we were ordered to Ras Tanure in the Persian Gulf to load oil for Rotterdam. The Suez Canal had reopened in 1975 and now, two years later, it had been cleared of block ships and dredged so that ships the size of the Silver Bridge could transit the canal in light condition only. In loaded conditions, we had to proceed around the south Cape.

We discharged the oil in Rotterdam and then were ordered north to tank clean and prepare the vessel to load a bulk cargo, as explained previously. We next loaded coal in Holland for Rio de Janeiro and then went down to load iron ore for Kobe in Japan. Then we went down to North West Australia to pick up a cargo of coal for Europe. On the way I was sent home on leave and was relieved off limits while passing Cape Town, on 16th September 1977.

While I was on leave I was asked to relieve a friend of mine on the coaster M.V. Polythene of Liverpool, an ex-ICI coaster (O.N. 183740, G.T. 330). I joined the vessel in Waterford and while I was there I heard of and applied for a job with Bell Line. After a visit to their office, where I handed in my CV, I was told that I would be hearing from them soon. We tramped around the coast and I finally paid off in Dublin at Bolands Mill in Ringsend dock, where we discharged grain from France into the mill. I believe we were one of the last ships to handle cargo in Ringsend Dock.

CHAPTER 20

Bell Ship Management LTD

DURING THE INTERVIEW I had with Bell Line they told me that they were building new ships and that, when they all arrived from Japan, Bells would be putting a month on-month off system of leave into place for the whole crew. In other words, there would be two crews for each vessel. Each crew would consist of the master, mate, chief engineer, 2nd engineer, cook/steward and four ratings. Nine people all told. This arrangement meant that the master and the chief officer had to do watch about but I liked the way it sounded and I agreed to join. I joined the company in November of 1977 and I never regretted it.

Bell Ship Management at that time, in 1977, was expanding its fleet and was having nine almost identical ships built in Japan for its container service between Ireland, the UK and the near continent. George Bell Shipping was an old Dublin company involved in brokerage and stevedoring. The company was bought out by Mr. George Holloway and the Bell Line name was retained by him. He was a man of vision and he inaugurated a container service from Waterford with chartered vessels. The service grew rapidly with the development of trade within the European Union and he decided to have his own fleet of dedicated container ships built.

From Waterford he then had a network of terminals, to and from which his fleet traded. These were in the river Usk just up river from Newport in Wales. Here, he developed an old dry dock and converted it to handle containers with a crane that straddled the dock and the ship. He called it Bellport. The company had the exclusive use of Victoria deep water berth in the river Thames at Greenwich and a purpose-built Bell Line terminal in Teesport on the east coast. Then there was the Rozenburg terminal in Rotterdam's Europort and another continental terminal purpose-built at Radicatel on the River Seine above Le Harve. He later opened a service from Newport to Bilbao in Spain.

On each terminal there was a control tower, similar to those in airports, which controlled the discharging and loading of the ships, the stowage of the containers in the compound, the loading and offloading of the trucks and trains, and the registering of the boxes and their positions. All movements in the terminal compound were computerized and under radio control.

On arrival in port the terminal managers and the chief officer worked out the next loading plan and if any alterations were required to the plan during the loading, the vessel was informed and adjustments made. With deck cargoes of containers the stability of the ship was crucial and had to be watched at all times. There was also a system where Bells handled all aspects of the transportation of the containers and where, if a company or an individual required a box, Bell line would organize the delivery, the collection, the customs and paperwork, the shipping and the delivery of the box to its final destination, thereby cutting out the middlemen and simplifying the whole business.

An odd fact about three of the ports worked by Bell Line, notably the Tees, Newport and Bilboa, was that each of them had a working transporter bridge. As far as I know these are the three last remaining transporter bridges still in operation. The first one I observed in working order was the Widnes/Runcorn Bridge which spanned the river Mersey and the Manchester Ship Canal, which has since been demolished since the motorway flyover was completed. These transporter bridges were constructed in the early years of the 20th century over rivers and canals, along which there was a flow of ship, boat and barge traffic and they could operate without interfering with that waterborne traffic. High pylons were built on each side of the river and canals and a gantry joined the pylons together at their peak. The gantry carried a carriage which was pulled across the river, backwards and forward by steel cables driven by winches. Hung below the carriage, at road level, and connected to it by steel cables, was a cage with a solid bottom. This was called a gondola, which had a steel and glass shelter built along the upriver and downriver sides to protect pedestrians from the elements. The centre roadway held vehicular traffic be it cars, lorries or horse-drawn.

In its loading position the gondola was winched alongside of the roadway and the waiting traffic and held into place by two hooks built into the shore end. Then the gates of the gondola were opened, as well as the gates on the shore end. First, the traffic would be allowed off and then the waiting traffic and pedestrians would board. The gates would then be closed and the gondola would proceed across the river with its load, provided that the way was clear of shipping. During dense fog the operations would be suspended for fear of colliding with a ship and the gondola also carried a fog horn in case it was caught out halfway across in a fog bank. This was the days of the industrial revolution and steam was king. Smog and fog had to be lived with and radio communication had not yet been developed.

Bell Line would also store the containers and deliver them when required by the owner of the goods and it was one of the first companies to computerize its operations. The company boasted that they could deliver a container to any place on the continent, the UK or Ireland faster than the post office could deliver a letter, and this was true.

I joined the Bell Line in November 1977 when the new vessels started arriving from Japan. They were all sister ships, were of the same dimensions (G.T. 1593.62, N.T. 982.71, B.H.P. 2100) and were purpose-built to carry containers. The containers had changed drastically since I left Fishers. The trade had flourished and the containers had become standardized with twenty foot and forty foot boxes being the norm, and two twenty footers could be fitted into the same space as one forty foot, thereby maximizing the amount which could be carried without loss of space.

Ships and the operations of ships had also changed. The ships were better equipped with modern gear, hydraulics and electronics. Hatches were hydraulic, bow trusters and Becker rudders were fitted to improve manoeuvring, main engine control was given to the bridge, improved radars and radio communications, and later on GPS and computers were also introduced.

Bells encouraged all their masters to do their own pilotage, wherever possible, and most had permits or were licensed to pilot their vessels in most of the ports except Radicatel where the French authorities refused to co-operate.

After some years, a 2nd Mate was introduced for safety reasons and this eased the load on the master and the mate. While running up the Thames we saw the construction of the Thames Barrier, the running down of the Thames shipping, the closure of the docks system and the virtual collapse of the British Merchant Shipping. It was also the Thatcher age and we witnessed the large scale destruction of the coal and steel trade and the redevelopment of the London docks while we went about our business around the coast.

At around this time, Bells decided to transfer their London operations down to Harwich. During my period with James Fisher I was a regular runner into Harwich harbour to Felixstowe. At the time we were the only company trading there, apart from British Rail and Trinity House which were based at Harwich Town itself. Felixstowe had changed out of all proportion since we used to load at the old seaplane jetty at Languard Point and it was now one of the largest container ports in Europe.

In 1991 Bell Line, launched the M.V. Bell Pioneer (ON 402544, GRT 5815, NRT 1927, KW 1927) in Japan and I was assigned to her when she arrived home to trade in Europe. She was of an innovative design and was a new concept of container vessel, with the bridge far forward and an open hold with no hatches abaft the bridge and with container cell guides extending above the hold coamings. Designed as a complete hatchless ship to sail under the Irish flag, the Irish authorities considered it to be too innovative and insisted that the bridge be shifted forty feet aft and for a hatch to be fitted forward of the bridge for safety reasons. They did not consider the complete hatchless ship concept a great idea and they compromised.

She was built rather like a floating dry-dock with the ends, instead of being open, blocked off. A bulbous bow was fitted on one end and a transom stern with an engine fitted on the other end. As well as the

First Hatchless Ship

usual fore and aft peak tanks she had side tanks up to deck level and was fitted with larger than usual double bottom ballast tanks.

All crew accommodation, storerooms and recreation facilities were situated in and under the bridge with the master's and chief engineer's accommodation on main deck level and the rest below deck. Her full crew complement was nine. The engine room was right aft under a very small docking deck space and completely covered in the hold at 'tween deck level, where containers were loaded on top. There were large capacity ballast and bilge pumps, which were estimated to be able to handle the largest amount of heavy spray and monsoon rain that she was liable to take down the open hold. Halfway up the hold and the ships side, there were large diameter overflow pipes fitted with non-return valves which in case of a pump breakdown, permitted any accumulated water in the hold to flow overboard when it reached a calculated level, without allowing the stability to reach a critical point.

As it was imperative that the vessel was upright at all times, when loading or discharging, so that the containers could slide up and down the cell guides, she was fitted with an automatic ballast transfer system that would pump ballast rapidly from one side to the other to bring the ship upright. A red and a green light was displayed in a prominent position on the aft end of the bridge where the crane driver could see them, if either one was lighting it indicated that the vessel had a list and the crane driver had to wait until the light went out before he could lower or lift the box. It worked well and I never saw the crane having to wait except when two or more cranes were working the vessel.

The Bell Pioneer was fitted with the latest equipment for navigating and manoeuvring with bow truster and Becker rudder, GPS navigation, electronic charts, the latest communication equipment and bridge control. Although we carried one engineer, the engine room was unmanned and covered by CCTV from the bridge where there was also a duplicate set of alarms and controls. The Wartsilla main engine drove the propeller and a shaft generator which supplied electric power. If there was a main engine breakdown you could reverse the polarity of the shaft generator, hook it up to the two generators, and turn the propeller and manoeuvre the ship by this method. It was strictly an emergency *get-you-home* system and gave you a maximum speed of five knots. I had occasion to call on it once, after we suffered a crankcase explosion in the main engine, and it worked. She was a lovely ship to handle.

During the period while the Bell Pioneer was under construction George Holloway sold Bell Line for an offer he could not refuse to a Dutch stevedoring company, with interests in German and South American ports. The new Dutch owners never changed a thing in the running of the organization, except to invest more money in the purchase of new containers and to continue with the completion of a new vessel which was fitting out in Japan. This ship was to be of a similar design as the Bell Pioneer, but bigger, and she was to be named Euro Power. She was also to be my next command.

In March 1993, in Hong Kong Harbour I joined the M.V. Euro Power (ON 402754, G.R.T. 6455, N.R.T. 1936, K.W. 3690, port of registry Waterford). After launching she was taken on charter by a South Korean company to inaugurate a new service between Korea, Taiwan and Hong Kong. Relations were not great between South Korea and China, or between China and Taiwan at that time and the Koreans took the opportunity to hire a neutral country's vessel to get this new trade off the ground. Times were changing at this time in the Far East. China was opening up for world trade and was preparing to take Hong Kong back from the British, who had had it on lease from the Chinese for the previous hundred years or so, and Korea, which was already an established industrial country, was anxious to get its hands on the new business that China was likely to create.

We were employed on a round trade from Ulsan and Pusan in Korea and then south to Keelung in Taiwan, then down to Hong Kong. From there we proceeded back to Keelung and to Ulsan, where we repeated the circuit. We discharged and loaded in each port and soon trade became very brisk.

In the Taiwan ports, we worked cargo under modern up-to-date container gantry cranes and berths with the ship stationary, in well protected and smooth water, where the cranes were able to work the boxes directly over the hold cell guides with a straight lift in and out. In Hong Kong we discharged and loaded while riding at a mooring buoy in the very busy harbour with a lot of motion in the water created by a large amount of passing traffic such as large ships, fast ferries and sampans of all shapes and sizes. The method of working there consisted of large square steel barges arriving alongside and making fast. Each barge has a large single swinging derrick crane, capable of lifting forty foot boxes of up to thirty tons weight on and off the ship, and of stowing up to twenty four of the boxes on board the barge and transporting them ashore. These cranes were operated by two people, one operating the lifting gear and the other person controlling the heavy guide wires. There was also mooring and spring wires from the barges in long drifts to the ship, controlled by more winches, for shifting and positioning the barge alongside.

Each barge was operated by a Chinese family whose home was also on the barge. The females of the family all helped in the working of the barge and it was common to see women working in the barge with babies strapped on their back and other older children eating and playing not very far from all the moving blocks, sheaves and snapping mooring and guy wires laid all over the deck.

Cargo operations at Hong Kong

View of cell guides and derrick barges Hong Kong Hr.

With all the motion in the water making the barge bounce off the ships side and the weight of the heavy crane boom, which was about sixty feet high, with a heavy forty foot box swinging from it took a great deal of co-ordination between the two crane operators and the deck crane guide man to get the containers into the slots of the cell guides. Very often the boxes would get jammed in the guides and a barge would nearly pull itself over while trying to free them.

All this action was going on with dozens of stevedores on top of the containers attempting to steady them while they swung them around and often missed their intended positions, while dockers raced to get out of their way. All this was going on board the crane barge as well. This was not a very satisfactory or safe way of working containers and damage to the ships side by the heavy barges with their sharp corners was serious. Damage to the cell guides in the holds, and to the containers themselves was also a problem.

In the Korean Ports, for some reason or other, two people used to ride on the spreaders the whole time the cranes were loading and discharging the boxes. Their job was to operate a lever, one at each end of the spreader, which turned the twist locks in each corner to secure and to release the containers for lifting on and off the ship. Four other men, one at each corner, guided the spreader into position on top of the box to be lifted out to enable the two on top to operate the twist locks. This was another highly dangerous practice, but at least the crane and the ship remained steady alongside the quay wall in port. Why the Koreans worked in this way I never could understand as the country was highly mechanized but it was prone to some peculiar practices.

We nearly always managed to get one night ashore on each roundtrip in Hong Kong, and one more night in Pusan and Keelung. It was a most pleasant charter to be on with an easily-kept schedule and had only two drawbacks: pirates and monsoons. Pirates were a serious worry in that part of the world and the best way to escape them was to keep the ship steaming at full speed and pray that you would not have to stop for repairs or such. That part of the China Sea is one of the richest fishing grounds in the world and there was always hundreds of fishing boats, of all shapes and sizes around at any given time. It was believed that a lot of the pirates were part-time fishermen, waiting around for a ship to drop into their lap. It was unbelievable the speeds that some of, what appeared to be clapped-out fishing boats, could get up to.

While we were out there, there were always reports of ships having been boarded by pirates, or vessels being hijacked and taken into little-known ports and the crews being held to ransom. The worst case that came close to us was when a small German container ship arrived in Pusan with the master and the first officer murdered.

Riding the spreaders in Ulsan, Korea

It was believed, among the shipping fraternity there, that the pirates were recognized by the captain and mate as being custom officers in their day jobs.

The last time that I had been through the Formosa Straits was in 1959, in the old SS Baron Murray and there was plenty of naval activity around then, which forced any pirates that may have been around to keep a very low profile. Now there was not a Navy ship to be seen on the horizon and the absence of any Royal Navy patrols in these waters made us in the merchant navy feel very naked in that part of the world.

Our other concern was the monsoons, which were seasonal, and the worst thing was to be caught in port when one hit the area you were in. In one blow in 1993 we were anchored in a small well-protected bay at Pusan in Korea, with about forty other vessels when we received a monsoon warning. I did not like the idea of being anchored in such a congested area where there would be little room to manoeuvre in the case of the anchors dragging, so I decided to get out to sea where it would be much safer. When I returned back to the anchorage, the day after the monsoon had struck, I found thirty vessels wrecked, some sunk when they collided with other vessels and others driven on to the rocks, with many lives lost.

On another occasion, when we were departing Keelung, which is situated on the very Northern tip of Taiwan, a typhoon warning was received alerting all ships, and predicting that the storm would follow a track north-eastwards up the Formosa Strait. On receipt of this message I decided to do something I had always wanted to but could not do without having a good excuse. I went the wrong way around Taiwan to get southwest to Hong Kong and avoid the centre of the hurricane but mainly to see the highest cliffs in the world and their cascading waterfalls. The water is so deep along that east coast of Taiwan and we were in so close under the cliffs that the monsoon passed over our head and we had a flat sea all the way to Hong Kong and arrived in that port twelve hours ahead of next vessel which had left Keelung before us. It added one hundred and fifty miles to the run but I was happy and our Korean Charterers were satisfied.

Typhoons are tropical revolving storms, which are called hurricanes when they occur in the USA and cyclones in the Indian Ocean, the Bay of Bengal and the Arabian Sea. In Australia they were known as Willy-Willies.

There was one thing that annoyed me about Keelung and that was the way they had of disposing of their rubbish. Almost every time when we arrived off Keelung we were made go to anchor off the port to wait for the berth to clear before going alongside. While anchored off, the sea around the ship was a mass of floating garbage, containing everything imaginable, including large amounts of plastic. I observed through the ship's binoculars, large flat-topped barges leaving the port loaded down with the stuff and bulldozing it overboard off the northern tip of the island and trucks dumping garbage off the cliffs into the sea.

On the trips north and south between Keelung and Korea we were able to observe garbage being carried north on the current from Taiwan. Taiwan is situated in a very important part of the world regarding ocean currents in the Pacific Ocean. The clockwise movement of ocean currents in the North Pacific Ocean flows west just north of the equator, from the Revilla Gigedo Islands off the west Coast of Mexico, and is called the North Equatorial Current.

The day after the typhoon at Pusan, Korea in June 1993

It then comes up against the Philippine Islands land mass, which diverts it north where most of it flows north along the east coast of Taiwan, but some of it is again diverted by the southern tip of Taiwan, and flows north up the Formosa Strait towards Korea and rejoins the Eastern flow at the Northern Tip of Taiwan. Off the northern tip of Taiwan there is a large eddy between the two current flows and the land, before they join up to become the Japan current. This eddy was the place that the Taiwanese Government used as a convenient disposable machine where anything that was thrown into it was carried around and around by the water in ever increasing circles until eventually picked up by the currents which flushed it all clear of Taiwan. That was their problem solved, but not ours. We, in the ships, were persecuted with large sheets of plastics and other debris being sucked in to the cooling water intakes and causing pumps and machinery to overheat, all of which had to be stopped, stripped down and the cause removed.

It was also a problem for many others, miles and miles away from Taiwan. From Taiwan the debris was carried north until it hit the south Japanese Islands where the current was split again causing a flow through the straits between Korea and Japan and another flow to the East of Japan. The Japan Current then became the North Pacific Drift and continues to flow in an easterly direction until it approaches the North American Coast, where some of it is diverted northward and is named the Alaska Current and southward, where it is called the Californian Current, which flows down the coast to Mexico, where it completes the cycle when it joins the North Equatorial Current again. So you can see that any large scale pollution off Taiwan, or at any other point in this large circular movement of water, can have very far reaching effects over the whole of the North Pacific.

I felt compelled to write a letter of protest to the Taiwanese Minister for the Environment. I was very much aware that I could be leaving the ship and/or crew open to Taiwanese government pressure, so I put off posting the letter until the ship had finished the charter. I received a reply from the Minister of the Environment, stating that he regretted very much that it was necessary to dump into the sea, as Taiwan was unable to cope with the waste problem at that particular point in time, due to the rapid expansion in industries and infrastructures, and that he was hoping to solve the country's waste disposal problems in the very near future (see letter below).

This was not good enough, I thought, although I did get a reply to my letter which is more than I can say when I sent a somewhat similar letter to my own government.

In December 2008, I read an article in a Nautical Magazine that there is now a huge problem in the middle of the North Pacific Ocean, where a large amount of plastics is captured in the massive eddy covering thousands of square miles, created by the circular motion of all the North Pacific Currents and centred in the region of Midway Island.

However, things were not working out so well on the home front. The Dutch parent company had overextended itself in 1991 and sold the fleet to a workers' management, backed by a Japanese bank. The new management had a cash shortage problem and to raise money they had to sell two of their vessels and so they began to look around the company for voluntary redundancies.

行政院環境保護署
Environmental Protection Administration
Government of the Republic of China

August 24, 1993

Mr. Daniel O'Neill
3 Abbeylands
Arklow
County Wicklow
Ireland

Dear Mr. O'Neill:
    Thank you for your letter of June 10, 1993, concerning the
floating garbage in the ocean near keelung. In order to improve
the situation you saw, we have constructed a new sanitary landfill
and closed the old one. We are also planning to repair the dike in
the old site in Keelung. In addition, we are implementing the Solid
Waste Disposal Project to achieve the goal of 85% properly treatmen
rate of domestic waste by the year 1996.
    As you may know, marine environmental protection requires much
effort from different approaches. In order to coordinate the effort
of different ministries, we are considering promulgating the Ocean
Pollution Control Act. Your concern about environmental protection
in Taiwan is most appreciated.

Yours sincerely,

Mr. Shih-Piao Ni
Directer General
Burean of Solid Waste Control

台北市10014城中區中華路一段41號 傳眞：(02)311-7777   41, Sec. 1, Chung-Hwa Rd, Taipei, Taiwan, 10014 R.O.C. Tel (02)311

Response received from Taiwanese Environmental Minister

Meanwhile, our charter to the Koreans finished in November 1993 and I was ordered to Shanghai to take up a new charter with the Chinese container company, OOCL (Oriental and Overseas Container Line), who wanted to start a feeder service between China and Japan. There was still ill feeling between the two countries, which began in the 1930s when Japan invaded and occupied parts of China, which lasted until the Japanese were defeated at the end of the Second World War. They needed to start the trade without rippling the waters too much and so they hired a neutral ship to break the ice.

China, at this time, was beginning to open up to the rest of the world for trade, and Shanghai was at the centre of it. It was a fascinating place with a lot of confusion and in a great hurry. The port and the Huangpu river, which flows into the Chang Jiang (the Great Yangtze River) about fourteen miles downstream, was crazy with the amount of traffic of all sorts. The noise was deafening, with every craft blasting away on their whistles and shouting abuse at each other as they passed, while sampans, with families on board, paddled their way through the busy waters ignoring everything.

We were given a pep talk by our agent when we arrived and he told us that there were three types of money in circulation. One was the official government currency which the agent was obliged to supply to us, and the exchange rate was crazy on our part. The other was known as the tourist currency which you could only use in government stores and outlets and where the prices were out of all proportion. The third was the black market, where every street corner had a dealer and for US Dollars you could get a great rate. But some of us were stung by the Chinese Spivs doing a runner down the alleyways with your money stashed away on their person. Having been caught out a few times all transactions were then carried out with the skipper of the ferry boat that brought us ashore. At least he was in no position to run. Our Filipino crew was the best negotiators, and almost all of our transactions were done through them.

The next thing we learned was that there were two types of uniformed police and a very large secret police force. One of the uniformed forces was allowed to drive through road traffic lights and the other wasn't. So you had to be very careful when crossing roads. The most amazing thing about the traffic was the millions of bicycles in use by the local people. You always had to carry identity, if you did not and you were stopped by police you were locked up. A walk up town was always fascinating and the large spacious promenade called The Bund, which ran along the city side of the river, was a favourite place to relax and watch the world go by. From here you could sit or stroll or jog, and observe the local people at their leisure, the large and impressive buildings left behind by the British, and what used to be the busy financial centre ran along the other side of the Bund, with buildings similar to the Liver building in Liverpool, which were now turned into hotels, offices and tourist shopping stores.

On the river itself, there was a constant flow of traffic of all description passing up and down which attracted a large amount of sightseers. The majority of the river traffic consisted of passenger boats which were always packed with commuters coming and going to and from the outlining districts around Shanghai and the numerous islands created downriver from Shanghai in the Yangtze Estuary by the silt carried down by the great river.

Across the river they were beginning to clear the scrub land and drive deep piles into the ground for future large scale developments. There was always people coming up to talk and to practise their English and they were often a mine of information. Behind the buildings along the Bund there was a different world and I often took a bicycle-taxi ride behind the scenes, so to speak, to observe the real world. On one occasion I came across a district where large bulldozers had moved in and started to level all the shacks in their path. It was an amazing sight, with people running ahead of the machines while grabbing whatever they could, including babies, in front of the advancing monsters. At the time, I had assumed that the people had been given no warning but I learned that they had been given a month to clear out, but unfortunately they had not been offered alternative accommodation and had decided to remain where they were until the very last moment. It seemed that that particular heavy-handed way of clearing the land for future development was not new and it was going on in a systematic way for some time.

One of the deals in the charter required that the name of the vessel be changed to OCCL Shanghai, but she was to keep Waterford as the port of register and the Irish flag. So here I was, shanghaied in Shanghai on the Shanghai.

We were to be on a regular run from Shanghai to Kobe and Yokohama in Japan, one roundtrip per week, with many parties, photo sessions and press releases with Japanese and Chinese charterers and clients, until the Kobe earthquake put an end to the charter. Meanwhile things were not going too good in the company headquarters with more ships being sold and another round of redundancies on offer. I was eventually asked to accept a deal that I could not refuse and so ended my eighteen years with the Bell Line and Euro Container Shipping.

About two years later, the company wound up operations amid a lot of confusion with sit-ins and court cases. It was a sad end to a once proud, well-run, far seeing and innovative company that was created in one of the worst financial periods of the 1970s and 80s, and had thrived. One of the reasons for the downfall was that all the ships were aging at the same time and needed to be replaced but the plan to replace them had run into money problems. While the ships were ideal at the time of being built, and all had been reasonably trouble-free throughout their life time, in the eighteen years since their launching the container business had changed, containers themselves had changed to suit EU rules in the changed length, breath and height of the boxes. It was easy to change the box but not so easy to alter the ships which had been built to suit a particular sized box. So, in 1995 I accepted a redundancy package from Euro Container Shipping PLC and amused myself golfing and sailing.

CHAPTER **21**

Yacht Marianda and the
Grand Canal Catastrophe

In 1980 I had purchased a 26-foot sailing boat from which I got great enjoyment, sailing out of Arklow on my leave periods. She was Fairy Atalanta with a midship cockpit, cabins forward and aft, swing keels, one on either side of the centre line and a lifting rudder on the transom. The swing keels and rudder, when down, gave a draft of five feet and, when lifted, a draft of eighteen inches. This system gave great scope and enabled me to go almost anywhere and dry out sitting upright. I had great fun running onto beaches and mud flats and getting into places where keel boats could never go.

The Fairy Atalanta was designed by Uffa Fox who also designed the fast rescue craft for Fairy Marine and the famous self-righting rescue boat which was carried under Flying Boats and dropped to downed air crews during the 2ⁿᵈ World War. These craft were made out of Ogba plywood, using the same system of construction as that which was used in building the Hurricane Fighters, and the Fairey Atalantas were built of the same materials left over after the war. They were also fitted with a small petrol engine, which I believe was a Steward Turner engine, most of which were replaced by a diesel engine later.

The Fairy Atalanta was the first trailer-sailer to come onto the market. This meant that it could be trailed behind a suitably powered car and launched any place where there was a slipway and enough water to float it. The construction method was as followes: the plywood was cut into four-inch strips, glued together diagonally over a mould in two halves and the two parts then fastened together to form a very rigid rounded hull, called a *Tumble Home*. There were no metals or pins used in the hull, all was glued, moulded and clamped together until set.

The lifting gear for the keels was the same worm type hand-operated gear used in the early fighter planes to lift and lower the plane's undercarriage. On the boats, the lifting gears were secured, one on either side of the heavy bulkhead which formed part of the mould when the boat was built, and which carried the weight of the mast. They were placed in such a way that one person was able to operate both keels at the same time. When lifted, both keels swung up inside the hull and into a specially built watertight box.

The boats were sloop-rigged and all sails could be controlled from the deep centre cockpit and were considered a very safe family boat. They were the first assembly-line built boats and the first trailer sailers, many of which are still sailing into the 21st century. The boat was very versatile and I have used her in a lot of different roles, such as sailing around Ireland while island hopping, pottering around locally, using her as a diving and swimming platform, picnicking with the keels up and, with the mast down I have travelled under bridges and up and down rivers and canal.

Forward of the cockpit was the main cabin with two berths, a chart table and instruments. The forward bulkhead of the main cabin was specially strengthened to take and spread the weight of the mast and keels and it also divided the cabin and the fore peak, which had shelves for storage and the hand-flushing toilet on a pedestal, stuck right up in the nose.

It was said to be the friendliest toilet in the yachting world. To be comfortable on the seat you had to open the hatch over your head and stick your head out. In that position you could hold a conversation with the person at the helm, or, if in port with anyone on adjacent boats or on the quayside; you could observe all about you.

Aft of the cockpit was another two-berth cabin which also held the steering arrangement. Each bulkhead was watertight and if holed in any one compartment and flooded the boat could remain afloat on the remaining intact sections. The engine was fitted under the sole of the centre cockpit with an eight foot, stainless steel shaft extending aft to the propeller.

1988 was the year of the Dublin Millennium celebrations and events were being arranged all over the city to celebrate the occasion. I had been a member of the Inland Waterways of Ireland Association for some years prior to the Millennium and one of the aims of the association was to renovate and reopen the Grand Canal which linked the river Shannon with the sea via the city of Dublin. After about fifty years of closure and neglect it took years of voluntary work and subscriptions to dig out the debris, repair the banks, and restructure the lock gates and walls.

However, they had it ready in time and its official re-opening was arranged to be part of the Millennium Celebrations and a flotilla of boats left the Shannon and arranged to arrive in Dublin in time for the opening. By the time the flotilla arrived, it had collected about fifty boats and they berthed in Portabello Harbour, a canal harbour, almost in the centre of the city. I was away at sea and I missed the re-opening by about a month but I was resolved to transit the canal on my next leave and spend a summer on the canal and the river Shannon with my wife and family.

I launched the Marianda, checked her out after her winter lay-up, and prepared her for the inland trip. I removed her mast and sails as they would be a hindrance to working on deck if carried and the mast would have to come down anyway to get under the many bridges. I carried a ten foot long plank to be used as a gangway and two twelve feet long alloy pipes to act as barge poles. I applied for and received a permit from the Board of Works, the Government Department responsible for the canal, and I received a lot of advice from them and from the Inland Waterways Association.

I was advised that I must arrive at Ringsend Basin in the Port of Dublin, where the entrance to the first lock of the canal is situated, with enough daylight left so as to enable me to proceed up the canal to Portobello Harbour and stop there for the night. I was also told that a lock gateman from the Board of Works would meet me at Ringsend lock with a key to open the lock gates and that he would accompany me up the canal until we cleared the city limits. This was all fine with me.

As I had previously cruised down the Barrow branch of the canal from Carlow to the sea at Duncannon, at the east entrance of Waterford channel, I was familiar with the operation of the locks and sluices, and I had my own lock key which I had to purchase in Carlow before leaving that town. This key consisted of a right angled piece of heavy steel with a square spanner-type flange welded to one end which fitted over the lifting gear of the sluice gates and which allowed you to lift the sluice open or to lower it closed. In all respects it was similar to a reel handle used on ships to wind mooring wires on to their reels. They were about ten pounds in weight.

So, I left home on the fourteen horsepower main inboard engine and with a one horsepower Seagull long shaft outboard, in case of emergencies. Well-equipped, I thought, for the leisurely trip I had in mind. I planned to stop off overnight in Bray Harbour and proceed early the next morning to arrive at Ringsend in good time to lock in to the canal and where I was to pick up Roisin and two young daughters who were to travel up overland. I duly arrived at Bray at high water as planned and tied up at the north quay wall, alongside a built-in ladder which I would use to access the quay. I noticed a lot of heavy machinery in and around the harbour and observed some construction disturbances on the slipway and the corner of the dock, about one hundred meters ahead of the boat. This did not worry me, as I intended to depart early in the morning before any work got underway. I went ashore for a meal and returned back on board at 10pm, just one hour after high water, and went to bed.

I was awoken at about 2 am by a horrible stench. When I went up on deck to investigate I found that the boat had taken the bottom and was in a channel which was scoured out by a flow of raw sewage pouring from a four-foot diameter pipe, ten feet ahead of the boat. I was stuck fast. I could not move or turn and there were ropes all over the place. There was nothing else to do only to get to hell out of this situation fast. All I could do at the moment was to abandon ship. So I got dressed and got myself ashore as fast as I could and spent the next few hours walking around Bray to keep warm, everything being closed at that hour, and strolling down to the harbour to look across at the boat, as it was my intention to depart as soon as tide had risen and there was enough water to do so.

As soon as I considered that there was water enough to manoeuvre out of the berth I went on board, holding my nose, and started the engine, let go the ropes and gave her a kick astern. Then the engine stopped and the boat came to a halt. I had fouled a rope. Normally, in a situation like this I would go over the side with a knife and cut. I was not prepared to go into that slime. I tried the engine ahead in the chance that the rope would fall off the propeller but it did not work out. I then hooked the rope with the boathook and cut it each side of the propeller, which freed the boat, but did not free the propeller. I then rigged the Seagull outboard and used that to get out of the harbour and into cleaner water where I intended to clear the prop. Just as I cleared the harbour entrance the outboard went into overspeed and lost its drive. On investigation, I discovered that the outboard prop had fouled the trailing rope which was tangled around the main engine propeller, which I had not yet had time to remove, and the safety spring on the Seagull had broken. I did not have a spare spring so I thought that I would get one when I arrived in Dublin and I set to clear the main engine prop.

When I had cleared the prop and got back on board again I started the main inboard engine which appeared to run alright until I clutched it in. In both ahead and astern there were a lot of vibrations. The shaft was bent. As the engine is amidships on the Fairey Atalantas, the half inch stainless steel shaft is about eight feet long, (2.5 meters) with about six feet of that outside the hull and through a "P" bracket just ahead of the propeller.

I dropped the anchor and thought about what course of action I was going to take. At the moment I could not use the outboard and I was afraid to use the main engine as I was scared that the whip in the shaft might spring the "P" bracket where it was secured to the hull and cause a leak. It could also damage the gland and tail shaft where I detected some movement and a small leak when the shaft was turned. I had enough canvas and spares on board to rig a jury sail. I did not want to go back into Bray where they were constructing a large sewage outflow. With the wind blowing about force three from the northwest sailing into Dublin bay was out of the question with the sail rig I intended to use. Going back to Wicklow was my best option, the wind and forecast was good, the harbour was easy to enter and I would be closer to home to do what repairs were necessary. I rigged the two alloy pipes as an "A" frame to form a mast, securing them to the deck and lashing them together at the peak. I also made a block fast at the peak to hoist a square sail using a long heavy oar, which I always carried for emergencies, as a yard to spread the square sheet of canvas which was normally used as a tent over the cockpit. I had an uneventful quite lazy sail south, close to the coast on a fair tide, and docked alongside the Saint Patrick, a Galway Hooker, on the east pier in Wicklow at 5pm that day.

After the episode in Bray I had decided to abort the voyage up the canal but the skipper of the hooker had a spare outboard spring that he gave to me and next morning I left early on the flood tide and resumed my voyage north again to continue on with my original plan to transit the canal.

The outboard pushed the boat along at 3 to 4 knots and I called into Dalkey harbour to purchase a spare outboard spring and to spend the night alongside there, before proceeding on the last leg of the journey to Ringsend. At about 1200 hours the Marianda was locked in to Ringsend basin and the entrance to the Grand Canal, where I met the lock attendant who was to open the locks ahead of me as I progressed up along the canal, as was arranged. He and I discussed a plan of action. I had already been advised by the Board of Works, when I collected my canal permit, to leave Portabella early and that I would probably be met by juveniles along the way and that the best way to handle them was to allow some of them to ride on the boat to the next lock and to make them agree to change at the next lock and allow a different group to take their place, and so on, in that order until we cleared the territory and that I might be able to get them to help me open and close the lock gates as we progressed along the canal.

The plan was that I had to get up to Portobello Harbour and stop the night there. I was to leave the harbour at five o'clock the next morning to get through the estates or townlands of Ballyfermot and Clondalkin, before the natives got out of bed, and that my attendant lock keeper would follow me in his car and have the lock ahead of me ready to enter until I was out of the Dublin area. Roisin and two young daughters, Niamh and Noreen, joined me at Ringsend, as planned, and we set off up the canal through the locks and gates with the lock gateman in attendance.

Right from the start I began to run into problems. This lower part of the canal, through lack of use, was full of weeds which slowed down the engine. In each lock, and sometimes in between locks, I had to lift the outboard to free the propeller, and this allowed us to make only very slow progress. My attendant informed me that the weeds above Portabello had been cleared by the Inland Waterways to allow the flotilla of boats down for the Millennium and that all would be fine after that.

I tied up at a convenient berth in the empty basin at Portobello, exhausted from climbing up the bank, swinging gates open and closed, opening and closing sluice gates, attending moorings and the outboard. Granted, I had some help from the canal attendant. He had the key. When we had settled I went ashore and phoned some friends (there were no mobile phones in those days), to come and visit us as we had arranged a small party to celebrate our first arrival at an inland port and the beginning of the inland voyage. I cut the party short as we had to be up early the following morning, which was a Sunday, and planned to go to bed early. But there was no sleep. As the boat was the only craft in the harbour the Marianda had become a point of interest to strollers along the bank. People kept stepping on board and rocking the boat, the deck being conveniently level with the quay wall, and as we were all turned in they all thought that there was no-one on board. Clearly this could not go on and, as it being a Saturday night, with a large public house on the quayside only a few steps away, it was only the beginning of things to come.

I shifted the boat about twenty meters directly across the harbour and tied up alongside a grassy bank inside the security area of the Ever Ready factory, which was there at that time, and made fast to the security fence which ran along the canal bank. There was no way anyone could get at the boat by walking along the bank without passing the factory security system. So we settled down again for the night. But that was short and was broken round about midnight when I heard splashes in the water and a lot of shouting. There was a group of inebriated swimmers, turned out of the pub after closing time, attempting to reach the boat, climb on board and swim back. A large crowd had collected on the quayside from which we had vacated and were encouraging people in the water and having great fun throwing others in while helping others out and then throwing them back in again. Others reached the boat and were unable or unwilling to swim back again as things were starting to get out of hand.

Soon the police arrived, then the fire brigade and next the ambulances. I ferried swimmers, who had made it to the boat, back across the dock where the police promptly commandeered the boat and me for a possible search and rescue mission. I and the boat were released at about 2 am. Fortunately, there were no fatalities or damages and the crowd dispersed. There was no sleep for any of us that night.

It was at this point that I began to have doubts about the wisdom of having chosen Dublin and the Grand Canal as a means of entry to the Inland Waterways and as a starting point for our holiday. Particularly as I had been warned by both the OPW and the IWA of the special attention we might receive from some local residents who we were likely to meet further up the canal. Looking back on events it occurred to me that no person in the OPW or the IWA had actually come straight out and told me not to attempt the run. I learned later that they were trying to encourage boats to use the canal again and that the gatemen had been warned not to advertise or display any negative feelings to users of the canal. I also discovered, much later, when I was exiting the canal system, that, when the flotilla of boats cruised down for the millennium, each boat had about four able-bodied persons on board and that there was also a group of guards hired from a security firm to accompany the boats as they negotiated the locks.

At five, I cast off and proceeded to the first lock to meet up with the lock gateman as agreed. But again, we were delayed due to the growth of heavy weeds in the water and on arrival the gateman informed me that unless I made better speed I would never clear the troublesome areas in time to avoid the interference that he knew we were going to experience. But we decided to push on as we had come too far and put up with so much to abort now. Progress up the canal got slower as a westerly wind, which was blowing directly down the canal, began to increase, and this, together with the weeds slowed us up more and more.

At about nine or ten o'clock the locals began to make an appearance and soon the word must have spread, for, before long, there was quite a lot of youngsters asking for a ride on the boat and offering all kinds of suggestions and advice. I allowed some on board and they agreed to get off at the next lock but when we got to the next lock they refused to allow another batch on to take their places and a mini battle commenced. I was beginning to lose control of my own boat and as I was ashore on the canal lock trying to open and close the heavy gates they were attempting to hinder me by pushing against me on the lever arm.

As we progressed slowly westbound up the canal against wind, weeds, interfering teenagers, and young children, I observed that the landscape was deteriorating as we travelled along. We had left the tidy homes and struggled through housing estates. Now, the houses were gradually moving away from the canal and being replaced by abandoned factory sites. We passed wrecked telephone boxes, vandalized buildings and obstructions of all kinds dumped into the canal and almost blocking it. At one point I saw a JCB hanging down the bank balanced on its bucket, stuck into the bottom of the canal.

At the fourth lock the gateman informed me that he would not be able to attend us after the fifth. He explained that that was the point where the canal veered away from access roads and he would have to leave his car unattended. He knew from experience that it would not be there when he got back to it. I then asked him if he would phone the police to help guide us through to the ninth lock after which, he assured us that we would be clear and into the open countryside. He replied that even if the police came to our assistance, which he doubted, they would only add to the problems and he advised against it. He departed us at 11 o'clock at the fifth lock and we were on our own after that and fair pickings for the gang on board the boat and on the canal bank. Some kept releasing the dinghy which I was towing astern. At another point I saw a young fellow running along the bank with the CQR anchor under his arm. When I stepped on the chain to stop it running out it almost went through his stomach. I then had to lock my crew into the cabins to prevent the hordes getting inside and running off with whatever they fancied.

However, past the seventh lock the crowd started to taper off and at the eighth lock they became fewer and more manageable. When we left there, we had no more passengers to cope with. I believe now that these young people, at that certain age, do not stray far from the nest and that the eighth lock was the limit of their territory. Apart from that, there is a long stretch from there to the next lock and, as we were making such slow speed through the weed, it was going to take too much of their time. Besides, they knew more than I did at that particular time. From the eighth lock there is a straight stretch for about half a mile and then you come to a slow bend. The banks of the canal from the lock to the bend are very low lying and at times under water and marked only by the long ten-feet high reeds growing along the banks in the swampy ground on either side. They reeds were too high to see over them, but looking back along the straight I could see the eighth lock in the distance.

It was at this point that we got stuck and I decided that it was all too much for me and my crew and that before proceeding further I was going to need assistance. I had arranged with my brother-in-law the previous day that I would call him and arrange for him to meet us somewhere along the canal and help crew for me. He waited at home all day for my phone call and I spent most of the day looking out for a working phone to call him. But they were all wrecked and mobile phones were not yet in common usage. So while the boat was stuck fast I managed to get ashore on the bank with the intention of walking ahead as far as I could to see what was in front of us. I had to force a path through the reeds and about 200 meters along the bank I found a clearance which enabled me to proceed a little further in the direction of the ninth lock and the appropriately named Ninth Lock public house.

But the clearance between the boat and the lock had been made narrow by a construction crew working on the planned new M50 motorway and an advance squad of workers was working on building a new bridge to span the canal which effectively blocked the canal at that point by the scaffolding and other materials. So, that was that, as far as advancing further was concerned, and I was compelled to return back whether I liked it or not.

I still had to get help to turn the boat and get it back to Portobello, our only port of refuge. I made it up to the public house and called the brother-in-law and he arrived down within minutes. I lost no time in filling him in on the situation. Leaving his wife to look after the car we made our way back to the boat where we found Roisin and the girls under siege by unseen vandals hidden by the reeds. They were able to see the boat from the locks, but as the canal bank had collapsed between the boat and the lock they were compelled to take a diversion to get to the boat, which was hidden by the high reeds, and they must have lost their sense of direction somehow. They were taunting those on the boat using abusive language and threatening to set fire to the reeds and burn us out. I found my wife, standing by with my loaded harpoon gun and diving knife and with the children shut in down below. This was really Wild West material and it was hard to believe that it was all happening about two miles from the centre of Dublin.

With help on board we lost no time in pushing the boat astern with the barge poles and found a break in the bank which enabled us to turn around and start back down. We got back to the eighth lock and I noticed a big fallout of the reception committee but I expected that they would be back in force by the time we reached the next lock when word got around.

As the wind was still blowing from the west and down the canal in our favour, I rigged the square sail again, on the A frame, and made great trouble-free progress all the way back to Portobello. We had to be ready to lower the mast and sail before entering the locks and while going under the bridges and it was not long before we got if off to a fine art. While we were proceeding back down through the locks there was little interference and I wondered what was going on and whether we were sailing into a trap. Eventually, I enquired as to where all the youths had gone and I was informed that there had been a nasty car crash in which three young joy riders had lost their lives and that they were all at a service for them. It's an ill wind.

We arrived in the harbour at about 8 pm and moored again inside the factory security fence and tried not to attract too much attention by our presence. We had a lovely, quiet, if anxious, night and after the work and trouble we had experienced we all slept well. It was hard to believe that it was still only Sunday. Next I contacted George Briely, the dock master at Ringsend, who promised and tried his best to arrange a gateman to assist me but, as nobody appeared by 10 am, I decided to push off on our own. It turned out that it was not possible to get a gateman at such short notice. We arrived at Ringsend at about 2 pm where George had everything laid on for us and fitted us into a safe berth for the night.

Only two incidents occurred when we departed Portobello. The first was when some kind person warned us that it was not advisable to allow my fourteen year old daughter to walk down the bank beside the boat as she was liable to be accosted by certain people on the bank below Leeson Street Bridge. The other was when an elderly little man, walking his little lap-dog along the canal bank, told me in all apparent sincerity that I would be advised to stop where I was and to be prepared to stay for a while because they had dried out a stretch of the canal for repairs which would last for months. He then just carried on walking. I was shattered. Nobody had mentioned repairs. I left the boat where it was and walked the rest of the way down the canal and found nothing amiss. What kind of a kick does a guy get out of that?

We reached Ringsend at 2 pm where we tied up in a secure berth and went home for the night exhausted. The next day I arranged to ship my mast, boom and sails up to the boat, re-rigged her and sailed out into the trouble free wide open sea. I took off from Dublin on my own, Roisin and the girls having had enough boating for that year, and sailed north into freedom. The main engine was still out of action, I had ordered a new shaft but it would take weeks for it to be delivered from the UK. Meanwhile I was determined to make the best out of what was left of my leave. I called at a few ports on the Irish side and then went across to the Isle of Man to Peel and spent a night each in Ramsey and Douglas. I then berthed in Port Saint Mary on the beach in the SW corner of the drying out inner harbour and beside the bus terminal, with the intention of staying for a few days in a lovely safe and convenient berth. Unfortunately for me, the wind went around to the south east and held from that direction for ten days trapping me in the harbour for that period as I could not sail out against the wind and could not use the outboard in a choppy head sea. From past experience I had found out that when the engine was lowered on its bracket from the transom it dipped under water and cut out when the bow of the boat lifted on a sharp head sea. A final touch to a disastrous cruise. Although I did enjoy my enforced stay in the Isle of Man.

In my view, the Board of Works, the Department responsible for the maintenance, had badly neglected its job and had done no weed or debris clearing since the canal celebrated its re-opening. They were not talking to the gatemen and had no idea that the canal was blocked above the eighth lock. The Inland Waterways were also to blame because, although they had put an awful lot of work into getting the canal opened in time for the Millennium, they had also neglected it after the event. Both had given me wrong information and both were working on outdated reports. They never mentioned anything about the security system that they had in force for the Millennium and gave me the impression that it was going to be plain sailing after we cleared the sixth lock. They allowed me to sail into a trap and to put the boat and family at risk.

About two months later I came across a beautiful little schooner berthed in Arklow. I noted that she was flying the American stars and stripes and was registered in New Orleans. She was about thirty feet long with a big beam for her length and built on the same style as the Chesapeake Bay Shrimpers. There were two people on board, a man and his wife. When I got talking to them I discovered that he had built the boat himself and that she was indeed a replica of a Chesapeake Bay fishing boat called a *Skipjack,* which are also built with a swing keel which enabled them to work the shallow waters of that bay, and in that respect was somewhat similar to my own boat. I asked the owner if he had sailed her across the Atlantic or shipped her across on board a ship. He told me that he had sailed her all the way from New Orleans which he had departed from about two months ago. I became very interested and I next enquired as to what course he had taken to arrive in Ireland. He told me that his trip had brought him from New Orleans up the Mississippi River and into Lake Erie, down the Erie Canal into the Hudson River, entering the sea through New York. He then worked along the north east coast of the United States and up the east coast of Canada and out to Newfoundland and then departed from St. John's to Ireland. When he reached the west coast he decided to travel up the Shannon from Limerick and then cruise east down the Grand Canal to Dublin and out to sea again.

When I asked him how he got on in the canal he replied that everything went better than he had expected. He said that he had been warned to expect trouble and that he was liable to be ripped off while going through New York State, which was not the canal I was talking about. I then asked him how he managed in the Grand Canal and he threw up his arms to heaven and told me that he did not want to talk about it. I then told him about my experience in the canal and then he opened up to me.

He said that all went well until he approached Dublin. He had attracted a fair bit of well-meaning attention from boat owners and other interested people on his trip up the Shannon and along the canal and it appeared the people were keeping a good eye on him and the boat as it approached Dublin. When the locals began to swarm on board, the people who were following his progress got together to help him out and protect his boat. He told me that it got to the stage when his helpers banded together and hired a crane and a transporter to lift the boat out of the canal and dropped him back into the water at Ringsend. He also said that his experience of his trip through Dublin had done more damage to himself, his wife and to the boat than any gales which he encountered in the North Atlantic.

Like me, his attitude was never ever again would he go near that canal. It annoyed me so much when, early next season, I came across advertisements in some yachting magazines, inviting boat owners to come across the Irish Sea and enjoy a leisurely cruise up the canal to the Shannon. I do not know which department was responsible for that advertisement, but it was obvious that they were not very well informed of the real situation. I told a friend of mine, who was also a subscriber to the Inland Waterways Association that if I ever again get the urge the tackle another inland voyage that I would be more inclined to choose, what could only be a comparatively quieter trip, to the upper reaches of the Amazon.

C H A P T E R **22**

Around Ireland in the Marianda

I HAVE GREAT memories of my leisurely voyage around Ireland. I attempted to repeat that trip, some years later, but had to abort due to bad weather that particular summer. For the first half of the voyage I had the company of my ten year old nephew, who travelled with me from Arklow to Sligo, where he broke his toe and had to go home. I had to resume the rest of the trip myself.

Leaving Arklow, in July 1995, I carried the tide down to Carnsore Point and, as the tide turned, I put into Carne Pier where I dried out alongside. We enjoyed a good meal ashore there and departed the next day on the west-going tide which carried us around the corner and then to the west. I first stopped off at the Saltee islands, which is a bird sanctuary and is uninhabited. We had to moor off on Billy Bates mooring buoy and row ashore in the dingy. Landing there was easy as the weather was fine and the bird life was fascinating. We spent the day exploring the island and watching its wide variety of sea birds that colonize the island, such as gannets, guillemots, razorbills and puffins, to name but a few.

On Prince O'Neill's Throne, Great Saltee Island

We left the Great Saltee Island and proceeded west and put into the lovely little village of Ardmore, in County Waterford. We sat the boat on the sand at the slipway under the cliffs and set off next morning for Ballycotton with its prominent island and lighthouse. As there are no islands on the next stretch of the coast, until we get to the Baltimore area, we spent the next night in Courtmacsherry and the following in Castletownsend where I paid a call to some ex shipmates.

It was not my intention on this trip to do long sea trips or night sailing, if I could avoid it. If islands were within easy sailing distance I island-hopped, if not, I would use the nearest convenient haven. I took a small diversion in towards the entrance to Kinsale harbour. I did not go in, as I had been in to Kinsale many times, and the harbour and town would be very crowded at this time of year. I liked Kinsale, its harbour and the waters around the Old Head of Kinsale. My grandfather fished out of there every summer in the early nineteen hundreds and up to the time that the Royal Mail steamer, the Lusitania was torpedoed and sunk by the German submarine in May 1915 with the loss of 1195 lives. My grandfather, Captain Jimmy Hagan, skipper of the steam drifter, the Dan O' Connell, was drifting for herring in the area at the time of the sinking and was one of the first vessels on the scene to help some of the survivors and to pick up bodies. While in that area I liked to imagine that period in time with all the fishing smacks steaming and sailing in and out of the harbour on their lawful business and then having to confront the awful tragedy of the sinking.

From the entrance of Kinsale, I sailed south along the Old Head land and into Holeopen East Bay to show my young companion how the bay got its name. About half way out along the Old Head there is a tunnel carved out by the sea and in the right position you can see under and through the head to the bay on the other side. My young mate was not content until I sailed around the headland to Holeopen Bay West and looked through to Holeopen Bay East and under the new golf course. There was good fishing in the West Bay and we got a nice few mackerel for tea before proceeding on to Courtmacsherry.

Our next island call after Castletownsend was to Sherkin Island where we spent two nights walking, sightseeing and enjoying the music in the pub. From there we took the short hop out to Cape Clear Island and spent three days there as it was larger than Sherkin and therefore took longer to get around. We first anchored in South Harbour and explored in the dingy and had many good walks ashore, and then we went around the island and tied up in North Harbour, where we watched the comings and goings of the ferry boats from Baltimore and Schull, discharging and then reloading their human cargoes of day trippers.

Up the creek and snug for the night

We then went to Long Island, off Schull, for a short visit and to have lunch in the comfort of smooth water. After Long Island we proceeded southwest and could not pass the lovely harbour of Crookhaven, where we stayed for two days in the small harbour drying out on the sand at low water and only yards from the pubs and restaurants. On departure from Crookhaven we proceeded through Dursey Island Sound with its cable car, the only connection the island had with the mainland. We passed through the Sound without stopping, as there was not a suitable landing place on the island and, as the wind was fair, I decided to set out for Bull Rock about six miles to the south west.

I would have liked to lower the mast and go through the tunnel, which has been carved out through the centre of the rock by the actions of the sea over the centuries, but there was a little too much motion in the water to risk it. Some years later I did manage to go through the tunnel in the fisheries patrol boat, the Bradan Bagha. From the Bull Rock we went across to the Skelligs to have a look at the beehive huts and the bird life. But unfortunately for me I had to stay with the boat as there was too much swell but my young mate did manage to land and have a quick look.

Our next island stop was at Valentia, which is in reality no longer an island, having been linked to the mainland by a bridge. But interesting never the less and it gave us a chance to stock up with stores and water in the small village of Portmagee. We then sailed across the mouth of Dingle Bay and in and then out of Dingle Harbour to see and observe the famous dolphin, Fungi. I did not go ashore in Dingle as it was too busy and I would have had to pay for a berth in the marina. I was determined to go around Ireland without using a marina, as I had the ideal boat to take refuge on any sheltered beach, cove or creek. So I went around the coast a couple of miles to Ventry and spent the night dried out on the beach and had a nice meal in the local hostelry.

Over the years, I had read a lot about the Blasket Islands, which had produced so many writers in its very small community. The islanders had all been removed to the mainland in the nineteen fifties due to the difficulty of supplying them and their houses remain in different states of dereliction. I knew the names of the owners of most of the abandoned houses, having read so much about them, and, having passed through the Blasket Sound so many times on ships, I had made my mind up that I would visit them someday. As there is no berth or quay and only a landing place between the rocks, I ran the boat up on the only stretch of beach on the islands and we had a lovely two days walking, climbing and swimming. The beach was named the White Beach by the islanders because the sand is almost pure white. It is also the only almost level place on the islands and was used by the boys to play football. That night we were the only ones on the island and it was so quiet and still it was easy to imagine the ghosts of past residents wandering around.

Our next island call was to the Magharees on the south entrance to Tralee Bay, which are a low-lying group of small sand and rocky islets with channels running between them, some of the channels drying out, where we were able to lay in peace, regardless of which direction the wind blew from. We had a great time fishing and searching the rock pools. We left there for the comparatively long haul to the next group we wanted to visit, the Aran Islands. We sailed over, close to Loop Head, then along the rocky coast to Kilkee. It was such a fine day that we looked into the town. Dropping the anchor off the shallow beach we rowed ashore to go sightseeing and do a bit of shopping for stores.

Kilkee, being a holiday resort with the beach crowded with visitors, we were scared to go too far from the boat and dinghy. I have always found that landlubber holiday makers had very little respect for boats and caused more damage in their ignorance and high spirits than anyone or anything else. So we cut our sightseeing short and, as it was good sailing weather, we continued on our trip. We sailed as close as possible under the Cliffs of Moher and very close to the famous Needle Rock, waving to the tourists and walkers strolling along the top of the high cliffs, until we came abreast of Doolin and altered course to pass Inisheer, the most eastern island in the Aran Group. As the only reasonable shelter is at Kilronan, on Inishmor, the largest of the three Islands, we made for there. We spent three days there, mixing with the tourists, walking, cycling on hired bikes, and generally enjoying the atmosphere, while the Marianda lay drying out on the beach well clear of the ferries and other craft and their wash. When we got tired walking and cycling we took cruises around the islands and making visits to various places if the weather permitted. As I had already observed the sea from the high cliffs of the fort of Dun Angus, I was particularly interested to observe Dun Angus from the sea below it.

Eventually we had to leave the lovely islands and their beautiful patterns of stone walls and proceed north on our passage. It was my intention to go next to Omey Island where I had spent some holidays, but the weather dictated otherwise and, rather than having a very uncomfortable passage around Slyne Head, I decided to cruise around Greatman Bay and Cashla Bay and to have a look into the new fishing harbour of Rossaveal quay. We took a leisurely sightseeing cruise around the bay and harbour, decided against going in to Rossaveal, as it offered little for the yachtsman, being too commercialized and busy with large fishing boats. We next went west across the bay and found a lovely berth at Sruthan where we went alongside a derelict pier in the creek. There were two old Galway Hookers resting on the bottom and lying against the quay wall. We went in ahead of them and examined the bottom in the clear water and found a soft smooth berth in the muddy sand alongside the pier where the Marianda soon dried out on the falling tide.

It was about six o'clock on a summer Sunday evening and we had something to eat before venturing ashore. Since arriving we had seen nobody so we decided to take a walk along the narrow road in a westerly direction and after about a mile we came across Carraroe Village where there was a festival taking place. We stayed and enjoyed the music and excitement. The next morning at about 0700 hrs, we cast off just before the boat took the bottom again and motored out to the entrance of the bay to see what the weather was like outside the sheltered bay. The weather was good for a run to Roundstone, so we set the sails and, with the wind on the beam, we had a good brisk run to Roundstone harbour.

On arrival at Roundstone we found a large collection of the famous Galway Hookers, some alongside but most anchored off the piers in the sheltered bay. When I enquired as to all the activity, I was told that there was a Hooker regatta getting underway the next day and that it was going to be run over a period of two days. So I figured that we would not be going anywhere for at least two days. After scouting around I found a nice cosy drying out berth in the western corner of the harbour and alongside a twenty foot high cliff and almost obscured from those above. When we dried out I went ashore to have a look around and found that we were berthed in the very centre of the village under the main street which had three pubs and restaurants along the row of buildings and shops, which faced out across the road overlooking the harbour, the bay and the beautiful views beyond the bay. From the street there was also a panoramic view over the course which the Hooker race was going to be run. On the sea side along the road there was a low wall to protect traffic and pedestrians from falling off the road and down into the harbour below. It was also the perfect height for sitting and watching the world go by. As the bars were only a few steps across the road, it was a favourite spot to sit while having your drink. There was music on in every bar and on some of the boats in the harbour. This was going to be a big event.

Marianda at Roundstone. High tide under the wall

When I went up and stood at the wall I knew we were going to be in trouble. Directly below me was the Marianda, high and dry for the next nine or ten hours, with the top of the mast level with the top of the flat wall and just beyond arms reach, with the masthead light, weather vane and VHF aerial making a very tempting challenge for the daring. It promised to be a hectic night. It was. There was not a berth to be got on the wall until well past closing time and you would be surprised at what people throw away thinking that it was all going into the harbour. There were bottles, cans, wrappings and lighted cigarette ends landing on deck for most of the night. In fairness to the people, the Marianda was difficult to see under the cliff, unless you leaned over and looked down and I think that there was no maliciousness involved, just thoughtlessness. As soon as the boat re-floated, I shifted berth to the far end of the harbour to enjoy the regatta.

Three days later, we set off in a northern direction again, by-passing Inishark to make up for lost time, and as the weather was starting to blow from the north west I decided to push on to Inishbofin, where there is a fine harbour, offering better protection. I was having a bit of trouble with the clutch slipping when the engine was revved up and when we passed Inishark I decided to take a quick look at the gear box to see if I could adjust it. We were sailing with n°3 jib and mainsail, with the steering in automatic. I lifted the cover off the engine which was under the floor of the midship cockpit. My young mate was asleep in the forward cabin and I, on my knees, buried my head and shoulders into the engine box. Then I heard the roar of a breaking sea on the port beam and the boat lay over to starboard on her beam ends. I was stuck with my head in the box, holding on to the engine while water poured over me and into the box. I thought we were gone. She then shook and righted herself and I managed to get my head and shoulders out of the box and found that she was still on course and had shaken the water off. There were about nine inches of water sloshing around in the engine box and the lee dodger was torn off its ties. Otherwise everything else was fine, except my young mate who had been woken from a deep sleep and wanted to know what I was playing at. We never experienced another sea quite like that again that day, and soon reached the harbour in Inishbofin.

*Marianda in foreground anchored in Cromwell
Harbour Innishbofin Island*

Cromwell harbour was named after the gentleman from England who, together with a group of same minded men, paid us all a visit in the 1600s and left their mark on every place they visited. It is a fine and sheltered harbour with numerous places to dry out and good walks ashore. While walking around the island I met an old gentleman who informed me that he had been taught to fish commercially by fishermen from Arklow in the early days of the century. The fishermen had been employed by the government of the time to teach the west coast people to fish from larger boats, prior to that the locals had fished only from their local craft, the hide or canvass covered, Curragh. He could still recall the names of many of the Arklow men, names with which I was familiar.

During our stay there I surveyed the narrow and rocky channel between the main island and port island on which is situated Cromwell's Fort. I decided that the Marianda, with her keels lifted, would be able to negotiate this rocky and slightly dangerous channel, so I waited until slack high water and brought her out and then back in through the channel. I wanted to do this because the channel is named Roisin's Gob, which is my wife's name.

Our next island call was to Clare island which was the headquarters of the famous Irish female pirate, Granuaile. Her ancient castle still dominates the entrance to the harbour. We had a nice stay on Clare Island which is becoming quite poplar for tourists. I was tempted to explore Clew Bay with its many islands but it would have taken too much time and I decided to press on north to Achill Island. It was my intention to go outside Achill Island but the weather started to deteriorate so I changed the plan and set course for the south end of the Achill Sound. It was an interesting and lovely trip up the sound on a strong flood tide with plenty to see and do. It was going to turn out more interesting than I expected for a very good reason.

When I suddenly decided to change the passage plan I did not have time to read the South and West Coasts of Ireland Sailing Directions thoroughly, which state that, "this sound, between the mainland and Achill, Ireland's largest island, is shoal for much of its length, with drying banks, but can be used in yachts of 1.5 meters draught at high water neaps. It formally provided a very useful short cut from Clew Bay to Blacksod Bay but now cables cross over the bridge so normal yachts cannot go through, each end of the sound provides a useful natural haven. It is rather difficult to go down to the bridge from the north but is more complicated to do so from the south and simpler to go from there to the excellent shop beside the bridge by motor dinghy or easier by car." So, in all innocence I arrived at the swing bridge and anchored in an eddy very close to the east end of the bridge and out of the strong tide swirling through the narrow channel, with a rope ashore just in case the anchored dragged.

After a while, when we had settled in the anchorage, I went ashore to look up the bridge operator to find out as to when he would next be opening the bridge. When I eventually found him, having been passed from one person to another, he lived beside the bridge, he informed me that the bridge could not be opened ever again as power and telephone cables ran across it as did water and sewage pipes, and that the bridge had not been opened for years. So I resigned myself to the fact and was prepared to spend at least the night there and to eventually retrace my steps and go back and around the outside of the island. As we were sitting in the cockpit having a meal and waiting for the boat to take the ground we were hailed from the bridge by a gentleman wanting to talk to me about the bridge, so I arranged to meet with him in the hotel when the boat was settled.

He asked me if it was my intention to go through the bridge and, when I told him of my discussion with the man in charge of the bridge, he told me that if I was prepared to hold on at the bridge for a day or two he would see what he could do about it. He informed me that he was a local solicitor and that he was chairperson of the local environmental group and that they were campaigning to have the bridge reopened and manned again to allow boat traffic to use the sound. He told me that it was their intention to make the bridge operational again and to create a point of interest to help boost tourism in the area and to recreate the safe passage inside the island for small craft, which existed before the bridge was built. He told me that the bridge was permitted to be built to allow road traffic to use it but, with a clause attached that it must be opened when required by boats transiting the Achill Sound and which they were entitled to after generations of use. But the County Council, who were in charge of the bridge, had a deliberate policy from the very beginning of discouraging boat owners and others from using the facility by applying delaying tactics and making complications. They constructed pipelines and cables across the bridge, instead of putting them under water, and effectively anchored it so that it could not be opened easily.

The chairman told me that they had asked various boats to stop and help them out with their cause but for various reasons all had declined, some did not have the time and other did not want to get involved in an argument with the council. I told him that I was in no great hurry and that I would wait and help out as much as I could and he went away to arrange meetings. The next day went with various meetings with various bodies while we, in the boat, were kept informed and entertained. On the second day, things were beginning to look up and I was informed that the council was having steel plates cut to blank off the pipelines and electricians organized to disconnect the electricity and phone cables.

On the third day all was ready for the reopening and all hands waited to see if the bridge would swing, having being closed down for so long. It shook and groaned, shifted a few degrees and stuck. It was then closed shut again and given another dart at full ahead and this time it did not stick but opened slowly with about four men oiling and greasing and applying heat to the moving parts. Meanwhile, a large group of people had gathered on each side to witness this reawakening. We were given a large cheer when we let go and, as I had been asked to clear the bridge as quickly as possible, because the island was without power or water until everything was connected up again, I did not hesitate. I drove the boat back down the sound to enable me to line up the opening so that I could approach it head on. With the mad rush of water, we went through the opening as if we were shot out of a gun. Had we misjudged the flow and touched the walls on either side, we would have been smashed. I had been asked to tie up on the north side of the bridge and join the party to celebrate, but I was unable to stop or pull up until I was shot through narrows called the Bulls Mouth in the mad tide. Rather than struggle back, I waved goodbye to all the people and continued on. I never heard how it all ended and I hope that the local environmental group managed to persuade the Mayo County Council to adjust their arrangements and to man and maintain the bridge and keep it operational.

While writing this in November 2008 I have taken great pleasure in reading in The Marine Times newspaper that they have formally opened a new swing bridge across the sound with much fanfare. I can only say more power to the local group of campaigners and I hope that the Marianda played a small part in their protest.

When leaving Achill Sound it had been my intention to visit the Inishkea Islands to the west of Mullet Peninsula, but the weather started to blow up a bit from the southwest and I decided to sail into Blacksod Bay for shelter. As I went deeper into the bay the wind kept backing to the south and to the east of south and kept increasing. I kept going north and the wind kept increasing until I found myself at the top of the bay and could not go any further. I tied up at the quay wall on the south end of the canal in Belmullet to consider my situation. I was wind bound in the very top of the bay.

Marianda on a broad reach

I could not hope to beat out against a strong tide and rough head sea. I was tied up at a non safe berth with a rocky bottom which dries out and on a falling tide with a run in the water. I would be aground in about two hours' time and the bottom would be shoved up through the boat by the motion in the water. The canal, which the British had constructed for just such eventualities, allowed small local boats to avoid the dangerous open water passage around the outside of the Mullet Peninsula, was closed to all but low hulled boats because some stupid ignorant people had built a bridge across it with a clearance of only about 2 meters. There was nothing else for it but to get the mast down and go under the bridge. This was not going to be easy and it had to be done soon. There was nobody in or around the quay as it was a very exposed spot and raining heavily and I did not have the time to go and seek help. The mast of the Marianda was not easy to lower. I had done it numerous times and it took planning and preparation. It was imperative that the boat remained steady and it normally took three men. First, the sails had to be taken in and the boom unshipped. Stays and shrouds slackened off and block and tackle rigged forward. Then the aerial and wiring disconnected so that the mast could be lifted out of the tabernacle. Lowering the mast safely was not easy at the best of times as the shrouds holding the mast central to the boat slacked off when the mast lowered it was normal to have a man on each side holding a stay each to keep the mast in the centre line. With myself on the tackle and my young mate guiding the lowering wooden mast and with the swell in the water I knew it was fraught with danger, but I had no option. It was either lose the mast or lose the boat. We lost neither but we did do some damage. The boat took a bit of a roll as the mast was down to about an angle of thirty degrees when it went with the roll and hit the curb of the quay wall. I secured the tackle and climbed the wall and then lowered the mast, while standing on the quay, with a rope onto the deck below. We then unshipped it out of its tabernacle and secured it horizontally to the pulpit forward and push-pit aft. I found that the tabernacle was damaged somewhat, but not beyond repair and nothing which a good hammer couldn't fix. I expected the mast to be damaged but on inspection I found that it was not bad, just scratched. The mast was the original mast supplied with the boat. Pear-shaped and made of wood it was constructed in two halves with the centre removed and then the two halves glued together, which in effect, made it hollow.

Some years previous, as I was lowering the mast for winter storage, I discovered that the glue holding the two halves together had broken down in many places and that they were slowly coming apart and allowing water through the joining and to accumulate in the lower part of the hollow core. This left me with no option but to take all the fittings off, separate the two halves and re-glue the lot. So I sought out Jack Tyrrell, the boat builder, for his advice as to the best glue to use and he gave me a pot of glue which was left over in the yard when they completed the building of the sail training vessel, the Asgard II. When the glue had well set and while I had the mast dried out, I bored holes at intervals along its length and injected the centre with expanding foam so that there would be no space left for water to lie, even if it did get through. Next I plugged and glued the holes and replaced the fittings. I believe that this job prevented the mast from breaking or springing when it hit the quay and that the foam in the core strengthened it considerably.

As soon as the mast was made secure fore and aft we lost no time getting under the bridge and through the 400 meter long canal and into the shelter of the harbour on its north end. Next day we went alongside the fishing vessel Marian, which I knew well, as she had previously been built and owned in Arklow, and used her derrick to lift the mast back into position.

We then sailed east along the coast to the seaside resort of Inishcrone where we dried out alongside the pier and spent a comfortable night there and next morning treated ourselves to a soak in the hot water and seaweed filled baths of the Victorian built sea water bath house. I highly recommend it. Feeling refreshed and well oiled after the bath we then proceeded further east to Rosses Point where we were contacted by the yacht club and directed to a mooring at Oyster Island. As it was a long bank holiday weekend the members agreed to keep an eye on the boat while we went home for a few days. While at home my mate broke his toe kicking football so I was going to be on my own after Sligo.

Back at Rosses Point, I collected my dinghy from the yacht club and on arrival on board I found everything as I had left it. I sailed north in fair weather and with an open mind with no deadlines or timetable and as I was passing Inishmurray island I decided to pay it a brief visit. I inspected the row of abandoned houses and the 6th century monastic buildings and then pushed on another bit.

Mullaghmore, which is almost an island, looked interesting so I decided to spend the night and dried out on the south pier. The harbour is well sheltered and dries completely. It's a large holiday resort with lots of activity. After spending a nice night there I sailed north past St. Johns Point and into Killybegs and cruised around the docks and berths before anchoring in the west side of the harbour in a small boat mooring area in mud and clear of the channel in quiet water. I rowed ashore and had an interesting tour around the dock, inspecting the various types of fishing boats, observing the port facilities and talking to the men involved.

The next morning I sailed around to Teeling harbour, having promised a friend in Arklow to visit his relations there. I duly arrived in the beautiful harbour and the first person I spoke to on the quayside informed me that he knew the man I was interested in contacting. Very soon that person arrived and introduced himself and made himself at my disposal. His name was Mr. Michael O' Boyle, retired school principle, and he entertained me with tales and stories of local history and events. He was a mine of information and he also assisted me by getting the clutch repaired by driving me back to Killybegs to an engineering workshop where he knew the man in charge. Many thanks to Michael.

I left Teeling harbour with the intention of stopping off next at Arranmore Island but again the weather deteriorated and, rather than proceed in uncomfortable conditions, I decided to find a safe haven in a convenient restful anchorage and relax. So I dodged into Dawross Bay and ran the boat ashore on the beach in calm and sheltered water just north of Rossbeg Village and enjoyed all the hotel facilities while parked on their beach, and the hotel guests enjoyed the novelty of having a boat in their midst, inundating me with questions about my voyage. I left Dawross Bay very early the next morning when the tide suited and before the hotel came to life and had a leisurely sail on the tide north through the rock strewn south sound to Aranmore Island.

On approaching the pier at Arran, at about 0830 hrs, I observed a lot of activity on and around the quayside and, as I got closer, I heard the sound of loud music coming across the water. I then picked out a gig rig on the end of the pier pumping out the noise and hundreds of figures gyrating, dancing and employed in various other forms of activities. As I lined up to go alongside a fishing boat I noticed a group of merrymakers break away and take an interest in Marianda approaching the berth and all offering to help. Rather than get involved with what appeared to me to be an out of control mob, I veered away and anchored off close to the pier to observe and to cook breakfast.

After breakfast I decided not to go alongside or to the beach inside so I went north around the corner and anchored close to the small pier inside Calf Island and the lifeboat mooring and clear of the crowds and out of the full blast of the noise. It turned out that a festival was in progress and that before I walked around to the harbour everything had quietened down somewhat and most people had retired to prepare themselves for another night of festivities. In the lull during the day I enjoyed a tour of the island and was not very impressed. I realize that I was not seeing it at its best, during a festival, but it could not compare favourably with the other islands that I had visited. I figured that it was situated too close to the mainland and too accessible and therefore had lost its individuality.

I left the anchorage early the next morning and sailed north through Aran Sound, past Bloody Foreland and out to Tory Island. There was no berth alongside its short pier due to ferryboat activity and the arrival and departure of local fishing boats, so I was compelled to anchor off and use the dinghy to land. I was lucky with the weather and the wind direction. Had conditions not been favourable it would have been impossible to go ashore. The island was doing a regular tourist trade with its new hotel and I walked its length and breath. It had some interesting features and views: the high cliffs on the northern side, the views south towards the mainland and the bare rocks of the east half of the island where the turf was stripped off, dried, and used to feed the fires of the potin makers during the war years when they carried on a very brisk trade.

I then sailed to Malin Head and entered the small drying harbour, near Ballygorman, on its east side where I spent the night dried out on the sheltered beach inside the pier. It's a very busy little harbour with numerous crab boats landing and lying up to four abreast and dried out along the full length of the pier. The fishermen appear to have a very good crab processing plant run as a co-operative and while I was there it was very busy.

I next sailed along the coast passing close to Portstewart, Portrush and the Giant's Causeway to Rathlin Island where I stopped for two days. I found Rathlin very interesting with its regular ferry service and its tidiness and quietness. Richard Branson had a project in progress restoring old warehouses on the dockside and the quays themselves. I spent hours sitting on Rue Point, the most southern point on the island, observing the famous tidal eddies which are caused by the tide racing around the point and changing constantly during the course of a single tide. I departed Rathlin on the first of the tide and carried it down to Carnlough, before the marina was built there, and enjoyed a quite night in the snug harbour. Leaving Carnlough on the first of the flood next morning, I carried it down to St. John's Point and then I cut across Dundrum Bay and into Newcastle under the Mountains of Mourne. Newcastle is another drying out harbour and I spent the night alongside the pier, close to the lifeboat house where I was entertained and helped by the crew and watched a video show.

On the way south, I called into Carlingford and dried out in the harbour and walked back to the Port of Greenore to renew acquaintances. Then I sailed down to Skerries for one more night and next day went out to Lambay where I was confronted by a huge sign on the landing stating that no landing was permitted. So that was my last island call. My next stop was in Greystones and then home to Arklow.

On approaching the piers at Arklow, I noticed a number of boats and the local RNLI Lifeboat standing off the piers, with some people lining the walls and I wondered what was up. At the same time I observed another yacht approaching from a more southerly direction. As we both converged, I discovered that she was the Gypsy Moth 11, returning to her place of birth for the first time since her launching and was sailing into a welcoming reception. I had the honour of crossing the bar with the boat, on which Francis Chichester won the single-handed race across the Atlantic.

Cheers, Marianda's Replacement

The round trip took six weeks and that was not long enough. There were many more places where I would have loved to visit or to spend more time in and I promised myself that I would do it again at a later date. There is something different about visiting small places in a boat compared to arriving there in a car, camper, caravan or as a tourist. In a boat there is always some person on the quayside to take your rope and to enquire as to where you have come from and where you are going to, what kind of boat, whether she is a good sailer and to offer you advice and direct you to the nearest services. Having had her for eighteen years, I decided to trade in the Marianda and purchased a fibreglass, 26-foot sloop named Cheers, with lifting keel. I felt that I could not give Marianda the attention she deserved as she needed a certain amount of maintenance every year as she got older and I sold her in good condition. Unfortunately, he new owner neglected her and she sank at her berth in Dublin. I examined her in Dublin at the quay wall where she was landed after being lifted out of the water by the Dublin Port and Docks Board and was left abandoned in very poor condition. Now in 2007, I still have Cheers from which I get great pleasure.

After finishing with Bell Line, I did a bit of relief work, on and off, as pilot at Roadstone's Arklow quarry jetty, a bit of fishing and amused myself sailing and golfing. Retirement was becoming a bit boring so, when I was offered a job, I took it.

CHAPTER 23

Bradan Bagha Patrol Boat

IN 1996 I was contacted by the Irish Nautical College and was offered a position as skipper of a fast patrol launch, the Bradan Bagha[8], that they were managing for the South West Region Fisheries Board. At that particular time, in 1996, there were big problems with illegal fishing for salmon all around the Irish coast, and in particular in the south west. Fishermen were using illegal nets of up to five miles in length which was doing an unsustainable amount of damage to salmon stocks and was also a danger to shipping, particularly to yachts that constantly fouled the nets with their propellers and hulls.

In fine weather and in daylight, the nets' small floats, strung out like beads along the surface of the water, might easily be seen by an alert lookout. In a rippled or rough sea they were very hard to see until you were on top of them and at night they were impossible to observe.

The fisheries' officers, or bailiffs, as the fishermen called them, were in a constant conflict with the poachers. Using shore patrols along the coast and in contact by radio with their colleagues at sea manning fast ribs, the fishery officers were beginning to hit the poachers hard. But then things got out of hand.

The Fisheries Board stored their ribs in a shed inland and it turned out that some person or persons broke into the storage area and slashed all the boats, destroying them. The officers were determined to hit back at the poachers and they borrowed and used smaller and inferior ribs in a surprise raid on the poachers. So, one day they launched the

---

[8]   pronounced bradawn baha, Gaelic for Salmon of Wisdom

boats and began to haul a large amount of illegal nets which their shore patrols had observed in the water. In their eagerness to recover the nets they overloaded the boats which turned over and dumped the officers and the nets into the water. At the same time the poachers were out in their boats, taunting and frustrating the fisheries' officers and refused to render them immediate assistance. Their idea was to let them soak for a little while to teach them a lesson. But by now, the officers in the water had become entangled in the nets which surrounded them, and those monofilament nets were deadly, and two of the officers died before the fishermen hauled them out. The whole exercise had gone completely wrong and turned into a tragedy.

As a result of this incident the Central Fisheries Board decided to upgrade the types of craft supplied to the fisheries' officers with something more substantial than inflatables, which were so easily put out of action by determined people and were not very suitable for the carriage of large amounts of confiscated nets. They came up with a design of a well-proven, forty-foot, twin-screw, high-speed, semi planeing inshore fishing boat. She had accommodation for six crew members, was fitted with a net hauler and carried an inflatable boat on the stern. There was a hold for the stowage of nets and the wheelhouse was fitted with the latest electronics which included radar, GMDSS, electronic charts and a scanner which monitored all radio channels.

As the fishery officers had no experience or training in the use of such craft, I was appointed as master and training officer after I had submitted a training program to the owners and managers. I took over from the builders at Crosshaven in Cork harbour, where she was built, and, with the help of a man from the builders I brought her up to Cork city quays to where the managers had their headquarters. I arrived in the city at about 7pm and went ashore for a meal. When I returned to the boat about three hours later I observed a lot of activity by police and security guards in and around my new command. I stood back and observed for a while before I approached them. When I inquired as to what was going on I was asked who I was and when I explained that I was the captain they informed me that I was never to leave the boat unattended and without a security guard and that there was a lot of people in that part of the country who wanted to see the Bradan Bagha out of commission by any means whatsoever.

This was the very first time that I had any idea of what might be in store for us. During the interview I had had with the managers they had not mentioned a thing about security problems or laid down any particular instructions, but only that I was to get the boat up to Cork and await orders. I learned afterwards that management was completely ignorant of this, as they were of everything else relating to the job, and that it was their first venture into management. The next morning the first batch of fishery officers arrived on board and hands-on training began.

For the first six weeks we were fully engaged in training the various officers who arrived in batches from around the country and for the next two weeks we were involved in showing the flag and making dummy raids on fishermen at sea and in ports to give them a taste of things to come and to show them how easily they could be caught. Our method of operation was to go to sea and disappear over the horizon. With our speed of almost twenty knots we could reappear anywhere in the southwest area in a couple of hours, or just sit it out and relax to keep the fishermen guessing.

When departing our base, which was shifted down to Haulbowline Navy Yard and under the watchful eyes of the Navy, we were able to monitor the fishermen on the radio and on their mobile phones passing on a warning to each other and this would continue after we had disappeared from their view. After that we would listen to a lot of guesswork as to which way we were bound. The very fact that we were at sea, whereabouts unknown, was enough to keep most fishermen in port but at the beginning you always came across some brave souls willing the chance their arm.

We often received information from spotters on the headlands and then we would proceed to the spot, out of sight from watchers on shore, and make a lightening raid on the offenders. By the time they sighted us it was too late and sometimes they would cut and run and at other times they might stay and fight. At first they might argue but later they took to using weapons such as slash hooks, boathooks and axes. There were rumours that some carried shotguns but I never saw any.

We were ordered not to get into physical contact with them but just to harass them, which we did. At times we would be hauling the train of nets from one end as the fishermen would be hauling from the other end. It would be a race to get the most nets on board before cutting. The patrol boat usually did better than the fishermen due to her superior manoeuvrability, larger net hauler, more crew and more working space.

Then we began to make night-time raids on the boats in harbour with illegal nets on board. This was very successful as regards the volume of nets seized but it could be highly dangerous as we could be sailing into a trap and we did escape narrowly from some.

As the fisheries' patrol boat was rather heavy on fuel, refuelling was a bit of a problem, as we were not allowed to refuel in the larger ports by harbour masters who did not want to risk any incidents between the fishermen and the bailiffs. To get over that we had a road tanker follow us and be on call to supply us at very short notice at various small piers or jetties and we would be in and out fast before the word got around and the protesters got themselves organized. The southwest coast of Ireland was ideal for this sort of intrigue and hide-and-seek with its numerous deep bays, inlets and creeks where you could gain shelter from any wind direction. Provisions were never a problem as we could easily take on enough supplies to last a week, which was our normal patrol period. Fresh water sometimes ran short and you watered where you could.

Landing confiscated nets had to be arranged and done secretly in places similar to those where we refuelled as it would not be safe to off load the nets in hard hit ports and amongst groups of fishermen. At our busiest period we had to land nets quite frequently as too many nets on board created a hazard. To receive the nets we had an arrangement with fishery officers who manned a truck and were on standby, similar to that of the oil tanker.

But the fishermen were beginning to get the message and towards the end of the salmon season fishing illegally began to taper off and we began to experience some quiet patrols. However, the poachers were not finished yet. When the season ended the boat was taken out of the water and put into her winter storage inside a large shed. When they opened the shed to make ready the boat at the beginning of the next season, they found her to be badly vandalized and put out of action for some time.

However I was not reemployed the next season due to dispute which I and another crew member had with the management. When the day came to pay off at the end of our contract we found that the management was not fulfilling the agreement in full and was refusing to pay us the agreed leave entitlement. We therefore shanghaied the manager and his runner on board the boat, moved out into the middle of the river, anchored close to the main road bridge in Cork city, put up protest placards and locked the management team outside on deck. I then phoned the local newspaper that sent over a reporter and took a photograph which they displayed on the front page of the next edition with the headlines "Pirates Take over Vessel in Cork Harbour". Needless to say, neither the boat's owners nor the management appreciated the publicity, resulting in owners appointing new managers.

On taking legal advice we threatened to take the management to court but they settled out of court and we got our full entitlement. We were never offered any further employment by the new managers.

CHAPTER 24

M.V. Nordstar

MY NEXT JOB was as relieving master on the M.V. Nordstar (G.T.470, built in 1978). She was a small coaster registered in Kirkwall, in the Orkneys. I joined her in Southampton and went light ship to Par, in Cornwall, to load china clay for Rotterdam and then loaded grain after completing discharging for Kirkwall. I was relieved in Kirkwall and I had a few days' holiday in the Orkneys and in and around the historical anchorage of Scapa Flow which I enjoyed very much.

"Nord Star" - and funnel, Oban, March 07

Nord Star

I next took a relieving job on the M.V. Kylemore in 1997. She was a typical German-built coastal tramp, owned by a German company and managed by an Irish firm. Registered in Cork her O.N. was 403108, G.T. 2563, and N.T. 1174. I joined her in Bilbao in North Spain and sailed to La Pallice in France to load grain for London. We then went from London back to St. Nazaire in France to load grain again for Hamburg. Then sailed from Hamburg to Kaliningrad in Russia to load fertilizer in bags for the west coast of France again and loaded grain back to Rotterdam. After this, we again transited the Kiel Canal back to Kaliningrad to load another cargo of bagged fertilizer for France.

We always had an argument with the shippers of the fertilizer in Kaliningrad about tonnage loaded. For some reason, which I never fully understood, the bags loaded on board were always five kilos overweight. Fifty kilos was printed on each bag while they actually contained fifty five kilos. They had some kind of scam going on but we had tallied all the bags as they had been lifted and stowed on board and we were positive of our figures. The ship was chartered to load 3000 metric tons and at fifty kilos per bag this meant that the ship was to load 60,000 bags, but at fifty five kilos per bag we were only able to load 54,545 bags when we were down to her marks. This caused a lot of confusion at first when we, on the vessel, were compelled to stop loading otherwise the ship would have been overloaded and I would have been liable to pay heavy fines. We, on the ship, had to sound again, all the ballast, fuel and fresh water tanks, check the bilges and the density of the dock water and do our calculations over. Still we found nothing wrong with our figures and we were baffled until someone suggested testing a few bags for weight. It was then we found that the bags were five kilo each over the stated weight. We explained this and proved it to the people concerned and, after much argument with dockers and cranes standing by, they agreed that the bags were indeed overweight but said that it did not matter since the charter was for 60,000 bags. I had to explain that the charter was for 3,000 tonnes and not for 60,000 bags and that we already had the 3,000 tonnes on board and that was it. So we left Kaliningrad with the shippers protesting, but it was all sorted out when we discharged the cargo in France where our tonnage was proved correct. When loading our second cargo in Kaliningrad some time later we had to go through the very same arguments but on this occasion we were not so concerned about our figures.

After talking to agents in France and to other seamen it turned out that there was some sort of racket going on in Russia between the shippers and the receivers. What exactly they were all trying to do and causing all the confusion I never could fully understand. This was the time of great changes where the old regime in Russia had collapsed and gangsters were rife and there were all kinds of scams going on.

The crew consisted of me as master, the mate and chief engineer were Indians, the cook was Filipino and the rest of the crew was Kiribati. While the Kiribati's were good seamen, they were like children when they got a few drinks. Kiribati is a comparatively recently formed nation which consists of a group of islands spread over a large area, situated north and south across the equator in the Western Pacific Ocean and just east of New Guinea. From 1916 to 1975 Kiribati formed part of the British colony of the Gilbert and Ellice Islands. It became independent in 1979. Most of the people are Micronesians, living on the many low-lying islands of which Tarawa is the capital. The total population of Kiribati is 62,000.

After the war a German shipping company started to call at Tarawa on its round trip to Australia to drop off small parcels of cargo and to pick up Copra and some phosphates, the island's only exports. They started to employ the odd native and eventually the Germans started a nautical training school on Tarawa to give the islanders some kind of income, but mostly, I suspect, to supply the German shipping companies with a cheap source of labour.

On one occasion I had one young ordinary seaman join the ship in Poland in late December when there was about two feet of snow on the ground. As this was his first time away from home and off his tropical island, he was completely disorientated and almost white with the cold. He had on only the clothes he had left home with and a small plastic bag. There was a supply of heavy working gear on board the ship to fit out new arrivals but, before he arrived on board, he was petrified with the cold. On Christmas day while in Kaliningrad, the crew managed to get hold of a few drinks. They then attempted to entice the two Russian soldiers, who were always placed on security guard at the shore end of the gangway in all Russian Ports, and who were always surly and non-cooperative, to come on board and join them for a festive drink. In their eagerness to get the guards to join them one of the crew fell off the gangway and into the freezing dock from where he was hauled out with the help of the guards. This seemed to break the ice between the crew and the guards for shortly after, one female sergeant did come on to have a stiff drink, while her partner went off to report the incident. When he arrived back he could not find his mate and came on board to look for her. He then decided to have himself a stiff drink and soon both guards became very intoxicated after they finished all the crew's booze, including all the sauces and vinegar on the table. They then fell fast asleep on the mess room deck and were almost impossible to move in their heavy winter gear and guns, so we all decided to let them sleep it off where they lay.

That was all very well until their reliefs arrived at their post and could not find hide or hair of them so reinforcements were called in to search the area and naturally the ship and crew were chief suspects. A squad of soldiers came on board and soon found their colleagues flaked out on the decks. After satisfying themselves that they were not murdered or injured and just drunk they commenced to kick and beat them up. They then carried them down the gangway and dumped them both in a snow drift not far from the ship where the lay for most of the night. I do not know what became of the two guards as we never saw them again and no information was forthcoming from their replacements. As for us on board, we were placed on ship arrest and were forbidden to step ashore for the rest of our stay in Kaliningrad; a sentence that did not unduly worry any of us.

We left Russia in a snow storm and again passed south through the Kiel Canal on our way to France, where we discharged the phosphates and loaded logs for Agadir in Morocco. We then sailed light ship to Foynes in Ireland where the permanent master returned from leave and I left the vessel.

Our visits to Kaliningrad coincided with the change in Russian politics and everyone ashore was going through a vast changeover with much confusion. People were walking around, factories had closed, ships and large deep sea factory trawlers were laid up. The only foreign currency acceptable was US Dollars. It was a dangerous place to go ashore.

CHAPTER 25

Westminster Dredging

MY NEXT RELIEVING job was as master of the W.D. Test. She was a Split Hopper Barge of 1543 GT, owned and run by the Westminster Dredging Co, registered in Southampton and engaged, together with a fleet of other assorted craft and dredgers, in the Middle East and based in Dubai in the Arabian (Persian) Gulf.

Split Barge meant that the vessel's hull was divided in two from bow to stern and hinged on the main deck forward and aft. Powerful hydraulic rams opened and closed the two separate sections of the hull, which allowed the dredged material to drop out of the opened bottom. There was a port and starboard engine room which also split with the hulls and each side was completely watertight as the ship was built in two parts and then fitted together. The accommodation block was built on wheels and runners and held to the decks by flexible brackets, which allowed the hulls to move on the hinges and to open up under the accommodation block, which always remained upright.

I joined her in Jeddah, in the Red Sea, which is the Port for the Holy City of Mecca in Saudi Arabia. We were employed in cutting out a new port about ten miles south of Jeddah and dumping the spoils, which consisted of rock, coral and sand, in a designated position some ten miles out at sea. Work was carried out on a twenty-four hour basis, with two crews on each vessel relieving each other every six hours and changing watches every week.

Jeddah was a horrible place to join or leave a vessel in those days, especially for heathens such as ourselves. I arrived there having been transported directly from the airport by a courier, who spoke no English, and dropped off on my own in a hut outside the harbour gates. All my papers and passport were taken from me by a person who told me to wait and then I was left alone without a word or a sight of another person for four hours. Then I was put in the back of a van and driven through the harbour complex and put on board a tug and brought out to the dredgers. I was very glad to find that a Dutchman was skipper of the tug, as prior to my arrival on board I had no idea as to what was happening. There were all sorts of things going through my mind as I waited ashore on my own and, without a passport, I could do nothing. The skipper of the tug informed me that he had been waiting two hours for me and that the treatment I had received was quite normal for the port of Jeddah.

Some time after I had arrived and had settled in, a crew member was injured on one of the other craft and needed hospitalization. The injured man was landed on the dockside in Jeddah very quickly and placed in an ambulance. It then took the ambulance three hours to clear the harbour area. Luckily, the injuries were not life-threatening.

I found dredging life very interesting and it was very well organized. There were three hoppers, including ourselves, engaged in dumping the spoils which were loaded into us from a large rock-cutting dredger. The dredger was a very sophisticated craft and highly computerized. Her suction pipe with the rock-cutter on the end of it was lowered from the bow to the bottom when in suction mode. There were two long jibbed cranes on each shoulder which swung out and dropped two anchors each one about forty five degrees off each bow. On the stern there were two *spuds*. These are large spikes about ninety feet long and three feet in diameter which are dropped straight down through a hole in the hull, pinning the after part of the dredger to the ground. This allowed the bow to turn from side to side in a sweeping motion with the suction pipe drawing the loose material off the bottom, while the rock-cutter turned on the end of the pipe and chewed up everything it came across, making it small enough to allow it to be drawn up the suction pipe, working away while being pulled to port and then to starboard by the anchors off each bow.

Meanwhile the two spuds on the stern were working in tandem pushing the dredger slowly ahead on hydraulic rams which gives cutting pressure to the rock-cutter while the anchors caused a sweeping motion forward and the pumps sucked up the loosened rocks and sand through the pipes and over each side into the hoppers for removal. The spuds leapfrog each other constantly, pushing the dredger ahead and the dredger's main engines power the huge suction pumps.

This method of operating meant that as the dredger moved slowly ahead, pushed by the *spuds* and at the same time pulled by the anchors from side to side, while the rock-cutter pulverized whatever material come into its path and the pumps sucked it up the pipe and discharged it into the hoppers alongside, all the time cutting and dredging a channel about forty meters wide and up to twenty meters in depth. To move the dredger to a different location or for whatever reason, the pipe, spuds and anchors were lifted on board, the derricks stowed, the pumps uncoupled and the engines used to propel the vessel to her new location.

The whole operation was self-contained and apart from the main dredger and the three hoppers, there was a repair vessel, one small and one large tug, two work boats, one supply vessel and one landing craft. As the dredger never stopped working the hoppers had to be manoeuvred alongside and timed so as to cause no delays and there was always two hoppers alongside, one loading and the other waiting to load while the third hopper was away discharging her load.

Supplies were sent out by container every month from Rotterdam and picked up by the supply boat which also supplied fuel oil to the fleet. No one ever got ashore for the period they were on articles, except for hospitalization or to go on leave. The contract at Jeddah lasted five months and then we took the fleet back around the coast to lay up in Dubai to dry-dock and await the next contract.

That came about four months later, when the fleet was sent across the Arabian Sea to the Gulf of Kutch, in India, to dig out a trench in order to bury a submarine pipeline under the gulf and through salt water swamps and marshes for environmental reasons and also for security. That job lasted three months and was uneventful, except for the intense heat in the enclosed waters of the gulf, between the high mountain ranges on each side.

We were then sent down to a small port south of Bombay in India to deepen a channel into the port so as to accommodate supply ships which were going to operate from there to a new oilfield off the Indian coast. We again brought the fleet back to Dubai when the contract finished for lay-up and to await the next job.

CHAPTER 26

Surveying Vessels, M.V. Siren

I JOINED THE M.V. Siren (ON 7616, GT 1425, NT 455, port of register, Kingstown) as master in Dublin, in January 1998. Prior to her being registered in Kingstown she had been the TSV Siren, a Trinity House Tender from 1961 to 1989 and built by Whytes of Cowes.

Siren, in her role as Trinity House Vessel with Buoys on deck

She, and one of her sister ships, had been purchased by a gentleman from Dublin, who was into survey ships at the time, and was interested in the Siren because of her diesel electric propulsion, which, because of its quietness while running, made her ideal for survey work. I believe that the sale was conducted on a *"as is where is"* basis and offers made by *sealed envelope* for the purchase of two sister ships in one lot. Soon after the sale was agreed, the gentleman from Dublin sold the sister ship to a person in West Africa, who intended to turn her into a yacht, and kept the Siren. I was informed that he received as much from the resale of the sister as he had paid for the two vessels.

The Siren was a fine vessel, as were all Trinity House Ships, but had one fault. She was a twin screwed vessel but had only one rudder. I have no doubt that Trinity House had a reason for that odd arrangement but it made her very hard to handle while berthing or manoeuvring at very low speeds. Twin engines with twin screws and twin rudders normally make berthing and manoeuvring easy, but with a single rudder situated amidships between the two propellers it can be a bit awkward.

When you wanted to turn to, say starboard, with twin screws you went ahead on the port engine and astern on the starboard engine with the twin rudders hard to starboard. Turning to port, you did the opposite, going ahead on the starboard engine and astern on the port engine, with the helm hard to port, without increasing the forward or after motion of the vessel. But with the single rudder, it was all quite different and slower. To turn to starboard while manoeuvring with a single rudder you went ahead on the starboard engine and stopped the port engine with the helm hard to starboard. This was because the back edge of the rudder, being in the centre and while in the hard over position, just touched the wash from the starboard propeller. This propeller wash on the rudder is the most effective way to get a ship turning while manoeuvring and almost stopped. If at the same time you went ahead on the port engine it would drive the ship ahead too hard but she would continue to turn to starboard. If the port engine was put astern it would retard the swing to starboard and slow down her forward motion.

When I joined the Siren she was fitted out as a survey vessel with a gantry over the stern and was on offer for hire. She had just been chartered by the British Ministry of Defence. We were ordered to Portland to be fitted with special equipment for the charter to the Royal Navy. The Siren sailed for Gibraltar for bunkers and stores and was instructed to rendezvous with the survey vessel Sir John Bristow somewhere east of Malta. While berthing at the bunkering berth in Gibraltar, in a breeze of wind, the Siren took a sheer to port, due partly, I suppose, to our lack of experience in handling a ship with such a configuration of propellers and rudder, and suffered a puncture caused by a spike protruding from a damaged section of the jetty. Repairs were carried out within a few hours and, after a night ashore, we were still in time to rendezvous with the Sir John Bristow off Malta.

We spent two weeks towing a torpedo-shaped *fish* at various depths and speeds, attached by a long wire cable through the gantry on the stern of the ship, with the Bristow monitoring from different distances and angles. We were never informed as to what the experiment was all about, seemingly everything turned out satisfactory, for after the operations we were ordered to Malta, with the Sir John Bristow, to wait while the results of the findings were checked out. Four days later we were given instructions to sail for Portland to offload the Navy equipment, after which we sailed back to Dublin to wait for further orders.

While in Malta on the Siren, I had the opportunity to visit the owner's other vessel, the turbo electric powered Blyth, which called there to be fitted out by the American company, Western Geographics, for a survey contract in the Gulf of Suez. She had just completed a contract for the Nigerian oil companies and was now chartered to the Arabs to survey close inshore for missed pockets of oil reserves, which they suspected were lying about undetected by previous surveys. The ship was fitted out with the latest equipment which enabled them to carry out three dimensional surveys rather than the previous two dimensional.

After I delivered the Siren back to Dublin I was asked to join the Blyth in her work area in the southern end of the Gulf of Suez, on the Egyptian side. The way in which the new owners acquired the Blyth in the first place is an interesting story. She was advertised for sale as the HMS Helga by the Royal Navy, on a *"as is where is"* basis, as she lay in Portsmouth. Bids were to be tendered in sealed envelopes. I believe that Hanley Marine Services had not put the highest bid on the vessel but, when the highest bidder was told to come and take her, he was not able to come up with the cash in the allowed timescale, and the sale was then awarded to the next highest bidder, who was Hanley Marine Services (HMS). They were given a very short period of time to come up with the money and to take her away. The new owners and the takeover crew were not allowed on board the vessel until the cash was on the table and then they were given a short period of time to get her out.

The M.V. Siren was in Dublin at the time, awaiting a new charter so the new owner took the whole crew of the Siren, thirteen of them, and himself, with a bag full of cash, across to Portsmouth and to take over the ship. Unfortunately, I had not joined nor even heard of the company at that particular time, but it is something which I would have loved to have been involved in. When the new crew boarded the vessel the Navy personnel, all forty of them, immediately walked down the gangway. There was no hands-on handover. The ship's name, Helga, had been removed from each bridge wing and all reference to her original name had been painted out by the Navy as she awaited a buyer while laid up in Portsmouth. Before departure the new owner had the new name, Bligh, painted on a couple of planks and hung one over each bridge wing and the port of registry, St. Vincent and The Grenadiers, painted on the stern.

HMS Harbour Master Portsmouth cleared the ship outwards for Dublin classed as a yacht and was so concerned that he insisted that there must be two tugs to assist in clearing the port before he would let her move. He also got one of the ex-crew members, who was an engine room petty officer and happened to be retiring from the Navy on that very day, to volunteer for the run job to Dublin, and the new owner to pay him for the job. I believe that all on board were quite happy with this man and they received valuable information and advice from him as regards to the main engine.

As everything on the ship appeared to be working and in reasonably good order after having been tested, the new owner informed the harbour master that he could see no reason why he should pay for tugs as the bowtruster and main engine were in good working order and he could see no problem manoeuvring the ship out of the berth. But the harbour master was having none of it. With all the expensive Royal Navy vessels and equipment lying about in close proximity and he was not on for taking chances so he paid for the tugs himself and bid the ship God Speed. The Bligh had an uneventful trip to Dublin but, when she arrived there, the manure hit the fan. Here was a ship with a dodgy, flag of convenience country port of registry, no registered name and no notice of arrival until they contacted Dublin port requesting permission for yacht Bligh to enter harbour. Some yacht.

The M.V. Helga was one of three sister ships built to Lloyds specifications, as a geographical survey and research ship for the British Government, manned and managed for them by the Royal Navy. All three of them were named after three Icelandic volcanoes. I believe that all three vessels served as hospital ships in the Falklands War.

I joined her offshore in the south-eastern end of the Gulf of Suez. I flew from London to Cairo where I stopped for about five hours in a hotel before I was awoken in the early hours and driven five hours across the desert and dropped off at an old finger pier and told to wait. The driver turned around and went away and back in the direction of Cairo, after indicating to me to wait. He never said what I was to wait for and, as I could see nothing only sea and desert, I could only assume that it had to be a boat and a small one at that, as it looked very shallow alongside the jetty. There was not a building or a craft or a movement of any sort to be seen or observed. The sun was beating down and I was feeling very lonely and vulnerable, especially as they had taken my passport at a check point somewhere two hours back in the middle of the desert where I was led to understand that it would be returned to me on board the ship at some later date after, it was examined.

About one hour of waiting and worrying later, I detected a very small looking craft approaching the jetty at a fast rate. As it got close, I could make out three people on board and I was relieved at first. Then, as it got closer again I could see that the men were all masked, with a large brimmed straw hat on their heads and all that could be seen was their eyes. The inflatable Zodiac dingy they were in had no name, just a number, and the crew were the nearest looking men to pirates I had ever seen. They came alongside the stone jetty at speed, one man hopped ashore, grabbed my bag and passed it on board to his mate and said to me "You captain for Bligh". When I nodded in the affirmative, he said "we go now" and indicated that I get on board. They were alongside the pier for less than three minutes when we were off again and when I tried to ask them where the Bligh was, all they said was "soon see Bligh" and the two hands promptly lay down in the bottom of the boat and closed their eyes leaving the remaining man at the controls. It was impossible to talk to him over the noise of the seventy five horse power Yanmar outboard diesel engine, roaring at full throttle, but the breeze it created was a Godsend.

Survey Ship Bligh, ex HMS Hecla, anchored off Suez

After about fifty minutes at a speed of about fifteen knots, we arrived alongside the anchored Bligh where I and my bag were landed on a pontoon under the accommodation ladder and immediately the zodiac which brought me there took off at speed to join a fleet of similar zodiacs buzzing around the ship at various activities. I soon learned that the zodiac which had brought me to the ship was one of eight inflatable boats carried on board and used daily for survey purposes and that the crews were all dressed and covered from head to toe to protect themselves from the fierce sun and dry wind as they had to spend about ten hours daily on board the open boats. Apart from the zodiacs the Bligh carried a small landing craft, a work boat, and two quad bikes on board and had also a small supply boat and what was called a gunboat in attendance.

The mode of operations was that the mother ship Bligh would anchor in a pre-arranged position and set up shop. A pontoon would be lowered over the side under the mid-ship's accommodation ladder to act as a landing and berthing platform. Then the zodiacs would be prepared for work at their stowed position aft on the helicopter landing pad, moved forward on their trolleys, along the boat deck under the midship crane and lowered into the water at the pontoon. The rubber boats would then take off and anchor about twenty marker buoys each with sensors and radio transmitters attached in a pre-arranged pattern from the Bligh. The gunboat would then steam up and down the lines of buoys setting off an explosive shockwave as she passed each buoy. The echo from the explosion was recorded by specialist men and equipment on board the Bligh and recorded three dimensionally on computers. Meanwhile the zodiacs would follow up retrieving the buoys/sensors and leapfrogging ahead of the gunboat, re-anchoring them until a square of about fifteen square miles around the mother ship was covered and of which she was the centre.

During this operation the zodiacs would be buzzing around like bees doing their job, reporting in and coming alongside to refuel the seventy five HP Yanmar diesel outboards, lifting back on board for repairs or to change engines and to transfer people from one area of work to another. The landing craft might be busy dropping off the quads ashore to cover the headlands, coral islands or sand banks, anywhere the gunboat or zodiacs could not get to, where the quad teams would set up explosive charges to be recorded on board the Bligh. The workboat would be employed retrieving anchors or transmitters which were lost or snagged on the seabed and various other jobs such as towing zodiacs or the gunboat back for repairs. By the nature of her job the gunboat was subject to a lot of punishment where the shockwave she sent out caused a severe pounding on the hull and which also carried through to the machinery and equipment.

The supply boat was used to keep us operational by supplying us in fuel, provisions, drinking water and stores. She was also used as a repair platform where she could haul the gunboat over the stern and do what was necessary. The helicopter garage was used as a repair shop by the mechanics for the maintenance of all small craft, quads and all other gear related to the survey.

Survey operations ceased at dusk when all zodiacs were lifted on board and overhauled, refuelled and made ready for the next day. Radios and GPSs would be tested and replaced by the electronic engineers and, before launching at dawn, the catering staff would supply all boats with food and water in insulated cold boxes to do the crews for the day. When they left the ship in the morning they were off for the day except for emergencies.

The electrical engineers had a workshop and storeroom under the bridge structure on the starboard side on the main deck, where they looked after all the electronics such as GPSs, VHFs, and computers, and other equipment that were carried and used by the survey team.

The ship was crewed by Filipinos, except for me. I had two mates and carried out four on eight off watches. I was in overall charge; the mate was in charge of all maintenance, movements of everything on and off the ship, quality control and all safety procedures. The 2nd mate was responsible for all safety and navigation equipment and charts etc. He also assisted the chief officer and myself, as required, and relieved the chief officer when he left for leave periods. I and my relief, Capt. Jack Byrne, were on a two months on two months off agreement with the owner. The deck crew consisted of thirteen men and a bosun. The engine room squad was made up of four engineers and an electrician, plus four greasers. The catering staff was made up by four cooks, six stewards, two laundry men and four catering boys. All Filipinos. The larger than usual galley staff was required, as the galley was open twenty-four hours per day serving meals during normal working hours and then feeding the workboat crews as they arrived back in the evenings and during the night feeding the night workers who worked throughout the night servicing and repairing the workboats and making ready all survey equipment while it was shut down for the night. The galley staff would prepare and pack the ice boxes with food and water for the workboat crews and store the boxes on board the boats and zodiacs.

Every job and operation carried out on board, from operating the crane, launching boats, lifting, shifting, rigging, painting and overhauling etc was given a work procedure which had to be adhered to. I have to say that the chief officer was excellent at the job, resulting in the fact that we never had a serious accident for the whole period I was on board the vessel, and at times there was up to one hundred people on board the ship, some of them greenhorns, and with all kinds of different operations and transfers being carried out daily.

There was a fully-equipped hospital and operating room on board, as befits a Royal Navy wartime hospital ship, and I, as the so-called doctor was responsible for the treatment of all injuries, infections and other ailments. Luckily I was never called upon to do more than dress wounds, give injections and distribute medications and sunblock lotions.

During the day, the bridge acted as the control tower for all craft movements in and around the ship and nothing was allowed alongside without permission. The Western Geographical personnel, scientists, engineers and recorders, all worked from a large room abaft the master's accommodation on the boat deck, about twenty men in all. This was where all the data was transmitted back to and where it was then processed and recorded. This room was jammed with all kinds of equipment such as computers and survey charts. The master's large dayroom was also used as a conference room. The rest of the ship's complement was made up of two Arab inspectors, two mechanics, four electronic engineers and thirty four boat crews. Ship's crew, boat's crew, cooks and stewards were all Filipinos and, apart from the two Arab inspectors, the rest of the Western Geographical staff was a mix of nationalities, the largest group being Americans. I remember one day, while watching a film in the smoke room, I counted twelve different nationalities: Irish (myself), American, Canadian, Australian, Bosnian, British, French, German, Norwegian, Danish, Brazilian and Filipino. With all this mixed bag on board we had very little trouble.

The accommodation was very mixed, my own being excellent, apart from my dayroom which had to be used occasionally for meetings. The chief and 2nd officer and the chief and 2nd engineer had single berth cabins below the master's deck. The rest of the crew were scattered about the ship in single berth and double berth cabins for the junior and petty officers. The ratings were accommodated in small dormitories of from four to six men, to larger ones of from sixteen to twenty men each. Overall, the accommodation was poor and crowded as can be imagined, considering that the vessel was built for the Royal Navy, and as such she was very seldom required to carry a full complement of one hundred people.

The food was always good and plentiful and never boring. The Western Geographical personnel were relieved every month on a staggered basis and were quite happy with their conditions. The Bligh could make seven tons of fresh water daily more than enough for all domestic uses such as laundry, washing, galley use, showers and toilets. All waste water was treated on board before discharge. Drinking water was supplied in bottles from ashore, no alcoholic drink was allowed and there was ample amounts of soft drinks available free of charge. An incinerator was built into the funnel on the boat deck which solved most of the waste problem. The waste that could not be burned was sent ashore in the supply boat for disposal.

The Filipinos were expected to do tours of at least nine months and up to one year. They were also quite happy at this arrangement as it gave them time to send more money home and to accumulate more leave. They also feared that, when their leave was over, they were sent to the back of the queue and never knew how long it could be. I understand that they could never guarantee that they could get back on the same ship, so that, if they happened to be on a ship which they liked for whatever reason, they might like to stay longer. I understand also that there was a lot of politics involved in the crewing agencies in the Philippines and that a seaman could be held back, messed about and abused by any little tin pot agent in the office for whatever reason.

In 1999 the Bligh was taken off station by the Arabs, due to a fall in oil price, and sent to anchor at Suez with a skeleton crew on board to wait for an increase in the prices. On my last tour of duty I re-joined her at Suez and after a month there we were sent to Malta to decommission. The contract was ended, after much talk and many meetings, to everyone's agreement she was stripped of all Western Geographic's equipment which was packed up and placed in mothballs. The ship was put in lay-by at the Malta dockyard and, after about a month standing by there, I and most of the crew were sent home. A stand-by crew in charge of the chief officer remained on board. They eventually brought her to Waterford where she remained for a long time and, after a few small contracts and another long lay-up, she was sold to Africa for scrapping.

My next survey ship was the Fire Hawk. She was built to serve as the Thames Fire Chief launch. She came to Ireland in about 1997 and was chartered by the General Electricity Company, who at that time were about to develop a wind farm on the Arklow Bank, about six miles east of Arklow piers. At first an observation tower was put in place on the north end of the bank and the Fire Hawk was chartered to carry out checks and to service the tower as required, bringing divers out to survey the bottom in and around the base of the tower and electricians to check and repair the instruments.

She was also employed to carry out environmental impact surveys, which included wildlife and bottom checks and also to find, inspect if possible, and plot on the chart, all wrecks in and around the bank and bay. Over the centuries, there must have been hundreds of wrecks in the area, only very few of which were known. Some we inspected but most were earmarked for further investigation and research. As there were electric cables to be buried on the bottom which would link up the wind turbines to the shore terminal, a track had to be plotted for the buried cable, so that it would clear and not interfere with any wrecks. I found that little job in the Fire Hawk very interesting in my retirement and I enjoyed talking with and observing the various people, the bird and wildlife, the divers and the surveyors, with all their different equipment and their work.

The Broadsword of Hornsby was one of four auxiliary sailing boats built for the Ministry Of Defence. One of each was given to the Navy, the Marines, the RAF and the Army to operate and to train personnel. The boats were capable of entering the Tall Ships Races. The Broadsword was purchased by Mr. Ken Hudson of Arklow and used by him to travel around the world at will. Built to accommodate twelve service personnel she was cutter rigged and fitted with all safety and electronic equipment.

I volunteered to help sail her as far as Gibraltar and four of us set off in October 2004 on the first leg of the owner's voyage across the Atlantic to the Caribbean, via the Canary Islands. The boat behaved magnificently in the gale of west to northwest wind, which we carried all the way from the Irish coast to Lisbon. It took us ten days from

Arklow to Vilamoura on the south coast of Portugal, where on entry we were informed that the Broadsword, known there as the Queen's Yacht, had been there some years previously and was entered into the marina free of charge. That was until they discovered the Irish Flag on her stern. We stayed in Vilamoura for a week and then carried on along the coast to Gibraltar. On our second trip, we set off before Christmas 2006 for Brest to load up with wine for the festive season. I am glad to report that both trips went off well with no serious incidents.

CHAPTER 27

Retirement

Now, in my retirement, I am enjoying my twenty-six foot sailing sloop. She has a lifting keel which allows me to go almost anyplace, with the keel up she draws only eighteen inches. She is also an ideal platform for my grandsons to swim and dive off and she sits up straight when beached. I also do the odd draft survey for various ships which load stone at the Roadstone Jetty which I can see across the Golf Links, about half a mile from me. I enjoy doing these surveys as it enables me to keep in touch with the seamen, the conditions in which they work and the changes taking place in shipping.

In 2007 the Arklow Sailing Club purchased a RIB for club rescue work and I had to do a special course on handling the craft and an exam at the completion of the course. I am glad to be able to report that I passed and received a certificate as to the effect.

In all I have worked on 80 different ships without counting the vessels which I have piloted in and out of Arklow harbour and Arklow rock quarry. You may wonder how I could have been involved in so many seagoing ships and boats of many different types and trades. When I passed for my Masters Foreign Going Certificate in 1968 it entitled the holder to take any vessel of any tonnage to any place in the world. It was an unrestricted certificate. In those days, there was very little difference in the working of ships and you learned about these differences as you went along. The *better* ship-owners liked you to join their company in a junior capacity and learn all about their trade and working modes as you climbed up the promotion ladder. It was also expected that you would be staying with their company for the rest of your working life, unless of course you or the company found that either one of you were incompatible.

Some young officers liked to look around and sample different companies at first and in general they settled for a company they thought might suit them and settled down with the intention of staying. The longer you stayed with a company the less inclined you were to leave. Others, like me, liked change and when I got bored with a company, a trade, a method of working, a type of cargo, a ship, or for whatever reason, I liked to move on.

In those days too, you could jump from a fishing vessel to work on a collier and from there on to general cargo liner, or a bulk carrier, tanker, tug, banana boat or whatever without any kind of specialist training. A seaman was a seaman and you were expected to learn as you went along.

Then things began to change in the early 1970s. Established shipping companies were going out of business, amalgamating or flagging out. Coasting companies were going to the wall and men who had thought that they were settled for life found themselves out of a job. What was worse was that most of the *better* companies could not care less about what happened to their previous *good servants of the company* and walked away from them. This was the cause of a lot of bad feeling amongst seafarers and changed their attitudes and feelings of loyalty. A lot of good seamen, sickened by the changes, left the profession and never returned to it.

Then economy of scale came into it. Crews became smaller. Larger ships were built; smaller ships sold off or scrapped. The Suez Canal closed and tanker tonnages went off the scale and most ships became specialized.

Now, I could not walk on board a VLCC, a tug, a supply ship, an OBO or a nuclear waste carrier or almost anything else without having previously doing a training course. You can, in theory go from one different type of vessel to another, but the fact that you would have to do a lengthy course puts most people off, which means that seamen are now more likely, more than ever, to be stuck on the type of vessel which they train for.

Since I started going to sea I have never been on a training course except one where Texaco sent me to Holland to attend a VLCC ship handling course. On the VLCC Texaco Frankfurt as chief officer

I was responsible for the deck operations of the Inert Gas System. In fact, when I joined her off Cape Town, I was the only person on board who had never witnessed an Inert Gas System working. No wonder the surveyors who later joined us in the Canaries were shocked to learn that I had never touched the system before or after the explosion.

Another reason for my changing from ship to ship, or company to company was the involvement of crewing agencies, reliefs carried out abroad by air, shorter sea time and more leave. When I first went to sea, we signed on for two years on foreign trade. You could sign off within that two year period, only if the ship happened to touch a UK Port, if not, you had to stay on for the period. Leave was at four days per month. Then it changed over the years until it eventually arrived at a one for one basis, meaning one month on one month off. This relieving abroad, the relieving by air transport and the fast turnaround in port time meant that it was not always possible to get back to your last ship. If you happened to be working through an agency you might even be sent to a different shipping company.

It's now a far cry from the days when general cargo ships got long spells in port, first discharging and then loading manhandling-sized parcels of cargo and where tramps spent often weeks waiting to get alongside and then weeks loading or discharging. Or when most ships carried a full football kit to fit out a full team. Or when the Padre organized football matches with other ships of all nationalities and with local teams. We once even played the inmates of the local jail in Mauritius. Then there were dances to go to in the Seaman's Mission and sightseeing tours organized and time off granted in foreign ports by the mate for your enjoyment. Granted, seamen being seamen, not everything always went off according to plan and even after a few loggings we all managed to have a good laugh about it all. But now, with the minimum crews carried and the quick turnarounds in port, you might just be able to allow a member of the crew a few hours off to get some rest.

Although seamen now get far better leave than we did years ago they now, with the fast turnarounds in port, do far more actual time at sea. And in this modern day crewing arrangements they are now more than likely, after their leave, to be sent out to join a similar vessel as their previous four or five vessels. The job has become more boring.

Marianda at Kilmichael Point, County Wexford

In 2009 I was elected Chairman and Curator of the Arklow Maritime Museum, a position which I enjoy a lot and which keeps me occupied.

Up and until 2013 I was doing the odd pilotage job in Arklow and Roadstone Quarry near Arklow.

In this year of 2014 I am preparing my sloop "Cheers" for the coming season when once again I can sail out of Arklow.